WITH CHRIST IN THE WILDERNESS

The Bible Reading Fellowship was founded 'to encourage the systematic and intelligent reading of the Bible, to emphasize its spiritual message and to take advantage of new light shed on Holy Scripture'.

Over the years the Fellowship has proved a trustworthy guide for those who want an open, informed and contemporary approach to the Bible. It retains a sense of the unique authority of Scripture as a prime means by which God communicates.

As an ecumenical organization, the Fellowship embraces all Christian traditions and its readers are to be found in most parts of the world.

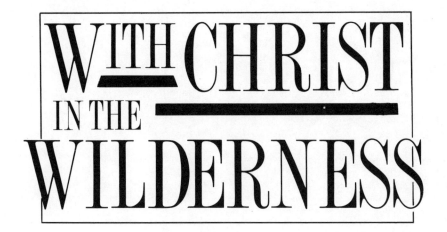

WITH CHRIST IN THE WILDERNESS

FOLLOWING LENT TOGETHER

DEREK WORLOCK and DAVID SHEPPARD

the bible reading fellowship
MAKING SENSE OF THE BIBLE

The Bible Reading Fellowship
Warwick House
25 Buckingham Palace Road
London SW1W 0PP

First published 1990
© BRF 1990

Bible quotations are taken from *The New Jerusalem Bible*, © 1985 by Darton, Longman and Todd Ltd, and Doubleday & Company, Inc.
Two quotations from the Psalms are from the version produced by The Grail, © The Grail (England) 1963, published by Collins in Fontana Books 1963. Some Readings have their introductions (*incipits*) as in the *Lectionary*, Geoffrey Chapman 1971.

Front cover picture: Tiger Design Ltd (Jerusalem to Jericho road)

British Library Cataloguing in Publication Data
Worlock, Derek.
  With Christ in the wilderness: following Lent together
  with Derek Worlock and David Sheppard.
  1. Lent – Devotional works
  I. Title.   II. Sheppard, David, *1929*–   III. Bible Reading
  Fellowship
  242'.34
  ISBN 0-900164-84-0

Filmset by Eta Services (Typesetters) Ltd, Beccles, Suffolk

Printed by William Clowes Limited, Beccles and London

Contents

Acknowledgements

The Scripture Readings throughout this book are taken from the *New Jerusalem Bible*, published by Darton, Longman and Todd, to whom our thanks are due. We also wish to express our gratitude to Miss Patricia Jones who has helped us greatly with the study notes and questions, which accompany the reflections for each week; and to Mrs Jean Jones for her long and patient work of typing, word-processing and bringing the text to its final form. Finally, we gratefully acknowledge the help of our chaplains and staff-members who have supported us in this initiative.

+ Derek Worlock

+ David Sheppard

Liverpool, November 1989

Illustrations

With Christ in the Wilderness

We hear much about the pace of life nowadays. Many of us are busy people, often running in order to keep up with the confusing demands of daily life. Though countrymen by upbringing, we both have for many years lived in a large city. With the passage of time, demands have grown more rather than less. Like all cities, Liverpool today presents problems which are long-standing and complex. To try to understand them is difficult enough, even before making a determined effort to solve them. Lent offers us a period when we can plan to withdraw a little, to make time to prepare for the great events of Holy Week and Easter.

With Christ in the wilderness we seek to renew the clear vision of God and his purposes.

In the Old Testament there is an intriguing inter-play between the wilderness and the vineyard. The wilderness, where the nation is born through the exodus from Egypt, is the place of Israel's first love for God. There the people of God hear his call to them with great clarity. They see right and wrong in stark black and white. They have a much clearer understanding of what is being asked of them. On the other hand, the vineyard is the picture of Israel, settled in the promised land, but in some ways the issues about how decisions must be made are less straightforward, more complex.

There is a great step forward in the process of civilization when people stop being nomads, settle down and build towns and cities. But with that settling down, life can become more complicated. A balance has to be struck. Case law builds up, and we learn to choose the lesser of two evils. A local culture develops, helping to shape the way people react in certain situations. Tradition evolves and takes the place of first-hand experience. The primitive simplicity of perspective in the wilderness is replaced by the more highly developed yet selective vision required in nurturing the vineyard.

It is the interplay between the vineyard and the wilderness which makes for so much creative growth in the Old Testament. God sends prophets such as Hosea, Amos, Micah and Isaiah, to remind Israel of their first love for him in the wilderness years. They stump in from the wilderness to recall God's people to fidelity and justice. Others like Josiah, Ezra and Nehemiah, try to reform and replant the vineyard so that it may be fruitful.

Jesus went into the wilderness immediately after his baptism in the river Jordan by John the Baptist. John, who stood in the long line of Old Testament prophets, was a wilderness person, calling unfaithful Israel to repent and be baptised, to start all over again. The approach of Jesus to his mission was different from that of John. The incarnation of the Son of God meant taking flesh, entering deeply into the situation of the people he had come to, and working out his Father's will then and there. Jesus loved the vineyard which he had come to reclaim for his Father. But his way was not that of John: 'For John came, neither eating nor drinking . . . the Son of Man came, eating and drinking' (Matthew 11:18). Yet both were rejected by those who did not like their message. Jesus himself pointed out that their critics were 'like children shouting to each other in the market place: We played the pipes for you and you wouldn't dance; we sang dirges and you wouldn't be mourners'.

Jesus made the point that, despite their different approaches, both John the Baptist and he were children of God's wisdom, doing his will. As a vineyard person, Jesus needed what wilderness people, like John, could offer. But at times he also needed to withdraw into the wilderness.

The wilderness tradition has always been alive in the Church; it has been maintained in the monasteries over the centuries. But it is not for monks and religious alone. Many other Christians see themselves as wilderness people: young people, fiercely critical of institutional life, whether of Church or State; poor people unjustly shut out from the good opportunities and the decision-making in the vineyard; sick and handicapped people with more time on their hands than they can use or would choose to have. As they question God's purpose in the world, all these are inclined to see issues of right and wrong with startling clarity.

A good example of this was a recent sixth-form conference on Christian vocation, which was addressed by a Christian business man who worked in the city of London. When he had finished his expected talk about the city and burdens of responsibility, he came under scathing attack from one of his young listeners who reeled off a long chain of scriptural texts about the love of money and greed. With passion the sixth-former went on: 'And don't tell us that, when we are older and wiser, we shall realize that life is complex and that we shall have to choose the lesser of two evils'. The boy sat down to a great burst of applause from his fellow students.

Being older ourselves and perhaps a little wiser than when we were sixth-formers, we know that there certainly are complex issues to face, that problems are seldom unrelated, and that choosing to respond to appeals for help from one group often leads to sharp criticism or the frustration of others. Seeking to follow our Lord, who took flesh to show us the way, means that we must be willing to take our place beside those who bear heavy burdens in management, be it of Government, schools, the professions or the business-world. We know that it can also mean willingness to stand alongside those who have no choice but to devote all their energy to the straightforward task of surviving the pressures which poverty and unemployment bring with them.

We hope that these short reflections on the Scripture Readings to be used during Lent, may be of help to individuals and small groups in their personal preparation for the celebration of Easter. They may, from the very fact of our having worked on them together, be of special interest to ecumenical groups. We have kept these latter in mind in preparing some questions as a basis for discussion and study together. May Lent prove to be the pathway to the one Easter garden of hope for all, whether wilderness people or vineyard workers.

Shrove Tuesday
Finding the way into celebrating Lent

For many people the season of Lent is little more than an annual reminder in a calendar or diary of a happening or observances of former times: rather like what seems to them an archaic reference to Michaelmas or Candlemas or even Trafalgar Day. Its significance is not to be ranked in importance with a quarter day or a new moon. It is difficult to say how widespread is such an attitude. Its existence is beyond doubt, and says something about the gap between whatever religious faith has been retained and the secular reality of daily life for many people.

The observance of Lent will vary in degree and intensity in accord with local culture and sometimes also with climate. In parts of Latin America, for instance, it is difficult to call for penance and self-denial, not only because of the hunger of so many people, struggling the year round to survive below the poverty line, but also because Lent comes at the height of what under normal circumstances would be regarded as the summer holiday season. For several Third World countries the equivalent of Lenten exercises falls more naturally in October and at Hallowe'en.

In Britain the second stint within the academic year is called the Lent term. It is the same with the law. Yet the Lenten liturgy in Christian Churches is often in marked contrast to life in the world round about. As soon as the Christmas sales are over, the focus for advertising shifts to the fertility of Easter bunnies. Glad of an excuse to side-step the demands of self-denial, people all too easily dismiss the whole business as being too commercialized to command reasoned assent. Instead they turn to pick up off the floor the summer holiday package-tour literature which has slipped through the letter-box.

Against such a background the Christian Church calls upon its members to repent their ways and to prepare for the all-important celebration of Easter. The call is for conversion: a turning from something and a turning to something: 'a time for losing; a time for keeping' (Ecclesiastes 3:6). In some cases the purging process may require all the forty days of Lent and more. To make a prompt start can be important. Time was when the frivolities and trivialities, with which we fill our lives, were punctually and annually set aside *before* the new beginning took place on Ash Wednesday itself.

In many parts of the world the finishing up of what is left in life's larder has become known as Mardi Gras. In Britain, with its rather more sedate expression of emotions, we still have Shrovetide. But elsewhere the spirit of carnival is uppermost and seldom confined to one day. To claim its Christian origin is one thing. Generally speaking, it strains credibility to try to attach any religious significance to much of the revelry which often fills the streets.

At times the scenes are almost Bacchanalian. The musical extravaganza, associated with Brazil, speaks little of the self-denial and virtuous living they are meant to anticipate. In other parts of Latin America, water-throwing is all the vogue, whether in exploding plastic bags or by the bucketfull. Visitors are well-advised to keep off the streets or to close their car-windows before venturing forth on a Sunday afternoon, before or just into Lent. It is argued locally that it is all good clean fun and quickly dried in the hot sun at that time of the year. Sometimes the water is far from clean. Most likely this curious practice is a relic, albeit an abuse, of the sprinkling with holy water, as with the *Asperges* of former times: a reminder of baptism and the washing away of sins.

Perhaps the most English of such seasonal celebrations is the pancake race, where contestants chance their arms in tossing the pancake on high from the frying pan, whilst moving at some speed over a measured distance. The true significance is however to be found more in the constituents of the pancake than in the fleetness of foot of the contestants. It is a good photograph each year for the news cameraman. The accompanying report seldom draws its literary inspiration from the egg, the flour, the butter and the milk, used to produce the object to be tossed on high.

If fasting is to be a mark of the Lenten penitential season, what more reasonable than to use up existent supplies of flour, producing bread, the staple food of life? The inclusion of milk, as an ingredient in the Shrovetide pancake, seems to suggest that its excessive use in Lent should be set aside. But the Butter Crosses in the market towns of Wessex are a reminder of those special pilgrimages of penance undertaken in past centuries by those seeking the indulgence of butter.

The greatest significance is to be attached to the egg itself, which speaks today not so much of the prevalent concern with salmonella, as of the new life with which our Lord broke clear of the tomb where his crucified body had been placed. In some northern districts the custom of egg-rolling on Easter Monday survives to this time. Almost certainly this must have been a celebration of the rolling of the stone from across the entrance to the tomb.

Before we celebrate the resurrection at Easter there are other mysteries to be observed. The previous year's palms, used to greet Jesus on his entry into Jerusalem, are burned to produce the ashes for the following Ash Wednesday. The egg, symbol of new life and resurrection, is tossed to one side to ensure a clear entry to the preparatory penitential season. So much for the pancake race. Far-fetched today, or yet another indication of the gap between inherited religious custom and contemporary experience? Perhaps the really important thing is to realize the need to lay aside those habits and weaknesses which may stand in the way of our penitential approach to the supremely important act of our redemption. Therein lies our hope.

The challenge for us is not so much 'churchy' observances as a determination to face the suffering in today's world, to shed the light of Gethsemane and Calvary upon it, and to bring to others as well as to ourselves the consolation and hope of the Lord's rising again at Easter. As the Jesuit Jon Sobrino has written: 'Lent is not merely a Church affair, or even just a Christian affair. It is a human affair. And if we dare not celebrate it, this is because something is wrong with us.'

ASH WEDNESDAY AND DAYS FOLLOWING

Your ancient ruins will be rebuilt;
you will build on age-old foundations.
You will be called 'Breach-mender',
'Restorer of streets to be lived in'.

Isaiah 58:12
Page 21

Low-relief wood-carving by Stephen
Foster, in Chapel of Reconciliation,
Metropolitan Cathedral, Liverpool
(The crucified arms of Christ
the 'breach-mender' bring together
Liverpool's two Cathedrals.)

Ash Wednesday

(Joel 2:12–18)

'But now – declares Yahweh –
come back to me with all your heart,
fasting, weeping, mourning.'
Tear your hearts and not your clothes,
and come back to Yahweh your God,
for he is gracious and compassionate,
slow to anger, rich in faithful love,
and he relents about inflicting disaster.

Joel 2:12–13

The name Joel means quite simply 'Yahweh is God', and the Lord Yahweh is the God of Israel. But the distinctive thing about the use of this title is that he is the *one* God. There is no other. All values that are not of Yahweh are false values. The pursuit of other values is false worship. So this call to come back to Yahweh, presented to us by the Church in this first Lenten reading, is the command to break with the false gods and other values which lead people away from God's law. The Lord of the covenant is our God and we are his people. We must renounce all that distracts or leads us from his truth; once more we must commit ourselves to keeping faith with him.

The falling away of God's chosen people and their subsequent return to him, often after they have been severely afflicted for having turned their backs on him, is in large measure the story of the Old Testament. In one way or another we can recognize in that sad swing of the pendulum of fidelity the story of our own lives too. Sometimes we see the folly of our ways because of some disaster we may have brought upon ourselves. At other times we recognize that our attempts to satisfy false appetites provide no lasting pleasure. We weary of excitement, the sweet taste of passing success can soon lose its savour. The return to the ways of the one God may be undertaken for many reasons. But its achievement will be through God's mercy and his desire to forgive. To use Joel's words, 'for he is gracious and rich in faithful love'.

Joel's call to repentance is made against a background when once again the people have failed to keep faith with God. Ruin has come to the land of Judah. There is a call to repentance and prayer. The harvest is lost, the vine has withered, a plague of locusts has stripped the land bare. The priests have donned their sackcloth, but self-pity and outward show are not enough. It is our hearts, not our outward appearance, which the Lord wants for himself. To turn back to him because of the fearful consequences of our stupidity and lack of faith is an inadequate motive. It is for the return of our love that he yearns.

So our return to him must be heart-felt and not just for self-interest. To be realistic, our turning back must be accompanied by genuine sorrow for our not keeping faith with him in the past. We have to face the question of how we have allowed his ways to be pushed into the margins of our lives as an irrelevance to the things which consume our interests. Lent is a time for repentance, but also for our honest examination of past failure: not to wallow in self-pity but to see where pride or cowardice may have led us in the past.

In all their enthusiastic and faithful commitment after the coming of the Spirit at Pentecost, the disciples must nevertheless have looked back often to their easy loyalty as they had made their way with Jesus through the palm-waving crowds lining the route of his entry into Jerusalem. With that they will have had to link their recollection of their betrayal and abandonment of him, when a few nights later he was arrested in the garden of Gethsemane. There are occasions in our lives too when our infidelity can, humanly speaking, seem almost as natural – 'it's what everybody does' – as our enthusiastic loyalty can seem at other times.

Our repentance calls for courage, faith and confidence in the one who forgives. Today, many Christians make ashes by burning the palms with which we enthused in our church on Palm Sunday last year. We are putting that moment of glory and triumph behind us; for the Messiah who rode the donkey, died for our sins an ignominious death upon the cross. In the ceremony of the imposition of the ashes, the sign of the cross is itself traced upon our foreheads, with the words 'Remember that thou art dust and to dust thou wilt return'.

Sadly, it is not only the frailty of human flesh that we acknowledge today, but also the weakness of our commitment. Some hard things are said quite regularly about the promises made by politicians and by others in positions of public responsibility. Some undertakings prove to be more difficult to achieve than to make in the first place. Such failure is by no means always the result of deceit. Keeping faith with another, or fidelity, has a wider application than the marriage bond. Political compromise, at the cost of principle, may seem excusable to the worldly-wise; but it all helps to weaken the value and importance of commitment in the service of the community. In personal relationships such a failure to observe a solemn pledge can lead to the breakdown of personal commitment and of family life.

Solemn agreements, once broken, are hard to restore. The beauty of our unequal covenant with an almighty God is that he is always ready to forgive, and to enable us to start again. It is with this spirit of repentance and confident hope in forgiveness that we begin our journey to Calvary and the Easter Garden. In this country at least we need not fear a plague of locusts such as the people of Joel's time experienced. Famine-ridden countries are seldom to blame for their situation, or for the hunger of their people. In our society the victims of AIDS cannot simply be identified with promiscuity. But there is affliction of various kinds in our world. We make efforts to raise funds for relief and research. Just occasionally we fast. But it is our hearts that the Lord wants, and he 'is all tenderness and compassion'.

> Lord, help us to keep a holy Lent
> by keeping faith with you at all times.
> Fill our hearts with sorrow for past failings,
> and with loving confidence
> in all you desire to make of us
> in the future. Amen.

Thursday after Ash Wednesday
(Deuteronomy 30:15–20)

> 'Look, today I am offering you life and prosperity, death and disaster. If you obey the commandments of Yahweh your God, which I am laying down for you today, if you love Yahweh your God and follow his ways, if you keep his commandments, his laws and his customs, you will live and grow numerous, and Yahweh your God will bless you in the country which you are about to enter and make your own. But if your heart turns away, if you refuse to listen, if you let yourself be drawn into worshipping other gods and serving them, I tell you today, you will most certainly perish; you will not live for long in the country which you are crossing the Jordan to enter and possess. Today, I call heaven and earth to witness against you: I am offering you life or death, blessing or curse. Choose life, then, so that you and your descendants may live, in the love of Yahweh your God, obeying his voice, holding fast to him; for in this your life consists, and on this depends the length of time that you stay in the country which Yahweh swore to your ancestors Abraham, Isaac and Jacob that he would give them.'

Deuteronomy 30:15–20

Today's Reading reminds us that Yahweh our God is the God of the covenant. The Book of Deuteronomy contains the principles of Moses, as given to the people at Mount Sinai, re-vamped over the centuries to fit their living in Palestine some six hundred years later. Israel had been unfaithful to the Sinai covenant and now must be led to believe that fidelity was for always, and not just when it suited them. This text is an encouragement to them to love God and to follow the commandments he had given them. The choice was theirs, but submission to his laws was the way to happiness; rejection of his ways was the path to disaster.

The commitment demanded of us in our Lenten journey is set forth quite starkly as a choice between life and death. If we are to surrender our hearts to him, in the way made plain to us yesterday, he will provide for us in every way we need. But we cannot be selective about his laws which we will follow, nor about the occasions upon which we will seek to do his will. Our choice must be based upon long-term commitment; it cannot be dependent upon convenience or passing gratification. To choose life rather than death is, under normal circumstances, plain enough. The real test is the application of that principle all down the line, to the lesser issues which we persuade ourselves are not so important, even trivial.

If yesterday the issue was whether to wash off the ashen smudge on our foreheads to avoid being a show-off or an embarrassment to others, today we have to face the small matters of daily life by which our integrity is put to the test. One of the difficulties is that we are seldom able to choose the issues upon which we should take our stand. It is sometimes easier to face penalties or punishment for refusing to conform on a matter of major importance, where clearly Christian teaching and fidelity to the faith may be involved, than to face ridicule for declining to go along with the crowd on an issue where, for example, Christian morality may seem out-of-date and in modern circumstances prudish.

Some years ago a member of the Cabinet found that in conscience he must resign from the Government lest he be party to a decision to cut back the grant towards the issue of free milk to school children. He was a man who over the years had dealt with decisions of the greatest importance, and would gladly have resigned in defence of his principles. In the end his political career was finished because he felt in conscience bound, even if reluctantly, to defend the free issue of milk to the poorer school-children of that time. He saw social justice as an essential part of his commitment to uphold God's laws.

The context in which we have to make such decisions is seldom one which concerns us as individuals alone. In issues which are personal and to that extent private, we come to recognize that decisions to give in on a matter, because 'everyone does it' or it is of no major importance, weaken the will for larger decisions in the future. In more public questions, undoubtedly public morality is damaged by the decision of a well-known individual to abandon Christian principles and practice, on the basis that his private life is his or her own affair. Choosing 'life or death' is a very broad choice, as today's reading suggests, and fundamental in its application to any situation.

Lent calls us back to walk in the way of the Lord. We have in fact, through our baptism, or through our coming back to its promises, already chosen life. It is not too much to say that by our fidelity we are sharing with Christ in the work of redemption, even in those smaller issues which we can easily let slide as of no real significance. To be able to choose is one of the riches of the human condition. We often say that poverty can mean the absence of freedom to choose. But where this fundamental choice is concerned, between life and death, between good and evil, between God and self, we know that the compelling attraction of what spells out eternal life is not a reluctant yielding to forces beyond our control. It is true freedom of the children of God.

O God of power and mercy,
help us to choose what is right,
and to cherish that freedom to choose
which you have entrusted to us.
May we always remember that our choice
may be important for others as well as ourselves;
and may it always accord with your will. Amen.

Friday after Ash Wednesday
(Isaiah 58:1–9)

Fasting like yours today
will never make your voice heard on high.
Is that the sort of fast that pleases me,
a day when a person inflicts pain on himself?
Hanging your head like a reed,
spreading out sackcloth and ashes?
Is that what you call fasting,
a day acceptable to Yahweh?
Is not this the sort of fast that pleases me:
to break unjust fetters,

to undo the thongs of the yoke,
to let the oppressed go free,
and to break all yokes?
Is it not sharing your food with the hungry,
and sheltering the homeless poor;
if you see someone lacking clothes, to clothe him,
and not to turn away from your own kin?
Isaiah 58:4–7

The prophet spells out that the acceptable fast has implications for social justice. Christians are not in the business of fasting merely as a slimming exercise. So Isaiah makes it plain that outward show is not enough. Fasting is related to that whole notion of turning back to the Father. In form and degree it may be relative to particular needs. It can imply a simpler lifestyle, and not just the wearing of less ostentatious garments. Linked with prayer and almsgiving it forms an inseparable trio, with each giving true purpose to the other two. But this extract from Isaiah takes us further, showing the importance of relating the penitential aspect of fasting to efforts to secure social justice: as when, for example, the amount saved by fasting, as a simple act of self-denial, can be devoted to the relief of hunger amongst the poor and the oppressed. This is the basic principle underlying several of the well-known relief and development organizations today.

To a great extent that is a contemporary use of the practice of fasting. Generally speaking, in the Old Testament, fasting, accompanied by sackcloth and ashes, was a sign of mourning and of repentance. Accompanied by prayer it was the accepted response to crisis. The prophets constantly warned against the danger of a mere external observance of the laws of fasting, without any interior involvement of the spirit. In the New Testament we find reference to prayer and fasting as the only answer to casting out the devil. With the same reasoning Jesus defended his disciples against that charge of their failure to fast, on the grounds that such a practice would be inappropriate to the joy they were experiencing at his presence amongst them. But he himself fasted for forty days before beginning his ministry. As with any penitential action, motivation was the key to its acceptability and effectiveness.

There is perhaps a danger that the penitential aspect of fasting may become obscured by the prominence attached to the importance of what used to be called almsgiving. If fasting is for a fund-raising purpose, it is sadly inevitable that some will fall for the simpler device of a cheque book and a subscription list. Once again the 'have's' will be able to fulfil their obligations more easily than the 'have-not's'. There are those who say that the only way in which the strong can help the weak is by creating more prosperity, so that some of the opportunities it creates may 'trickle down' to the disadvantaged. Today's verses suggest much more direct action on behalf of the poor.

Even in the relatively affluent society in which those in Western Europe live today, there is still no shortage of examples of homelessness. We are citizens of one world, and that part of the globe we call the Third World is subject to both hunger and poverty. But it is oppression which bears most heavily on today's afflicted. Last year, whilst visiting the township of Soweto in South Africa, we were told by a nun, working amongst those who were living in the most appalling housing conditions, 'It's not so much the poverty; people can get over that. It's the oppression.' Cruel divisions and discrimination exist in our world today. We saw almost biblical scenes enacted in those deeply moving pictures of starvation and disease during the famine in Ethiopia, at least partly brought about by a bitter civil war.

Today's extract from Isaiah provides more than enough justification for the concern of the Church for social justice. There are those who restrict their notion of immorality to sexual sins. Scripture like today's reading rejects such selective morality. Both of us try in our regular preaching and writing to name and challenge both personal and corporate sinfulness. There is notably less press interest in a sermon on chastity, or on reverence for parents, than there would be in an address on unemployment or housing.

Nevertheless we must be careful lest focus today be solely on the pragmatic or economic aspects of fasting, to the neglect of its penitential value. Penitence is asked of us for both personal and social sin.

Heavenly Father,
source of all mercy and forgiveness,
in your great bounty towards us,
grant that the fruits of our self-denial
may bring comfort and strength
to those who are in need:
and all for your love's sake. Amen.

Saturday after Ash Wednesday

(Isaiah 58:9–14)

If you deprive yourself for the hungry
and satisfy the needs of the afflicted,
your light will rise in the darkness,
and your darkest hour will be like noon.
Yahweh will always guide you,
will satisfy your needs in the scorched land;
he will give strength to your bones
and you will be like a watered garden,
like a flowing spring
whose waters never run dry.
Your ancient ruins will be rebuilt;
you will build on age-old foundations.
You will be called 'Breach-mender',
'Restorer of streets to be lived in'.

Isaiah 58:10–12

After the dire warnings of yesterday, the prophet Isaiah brings us today pictures of the hoped-for consequences of our fidelity to the call of self-denial and the service of those in need. It is a nice thought that if we will engage in genuine fasting, and to good purpose, we shall become like a 'watered garden'. Anyone who has engaged in the difficult work of reconciliation will also rejoice in the other title offered by the prophet, that of 'breach-mender'.

What likeness can we bear to a watered garden, and who or what will take the form of a watering can? The water itself must be God's grace, but it will be our attempts through personal self-denial to bring help to the afflicted which will lead us to the tap. We have learned to recognize the arid, cracked and parched earth in the sun-scorched land where there is drought. With thankfulness we contrast this with the beauty of an English country garden, with the myriad colours of its blooms spread like a patchwork carpet to the glory of the Creator. But in all honesty we also know how much work goes into the preparation of such a garden, the care which must be taken to water it, or ensure that it is watered if the owner or gardener is away.

One of the best features of an English country garden is the number of different flowers and shrubs which, given adequate soil and water, will grow happily alongside one another. Their variety contributes to the beauty of the scene. We can apply this truth to the variety of gifts which St Paul points out exists amongst God's people. They too have to be cared for, no one of them allowed to flourish at the expense of another. But the difference between the human race and the flower-bed is of course free will and responsibility. The gardener will tend the plants which may seem at times to threaten one another. The individual man or woman has to have regard for others and, if necessary, accept deprivation in order that the neighbours may have what is theirs in justice and in charity.

That is the ideal. We know that in practice, when there is enmity or opposition, the intervention of a third party, or reconciler, is needed. Some conflicts may call for recourse to ACAS, the industrial arbitration service. For others there may need to be the intervention of someone who is acceptable to both parties. Occasionally a peaceful solution may have to be enforced on unwilling opponents, but it would be hard to call such an enforced truce reconciliation.

We have both had experience of being asked to help to achieve a just settlement to an industrial dispute, or to take the chair at a reconciliation meeting designed to ease racial tension. This is due more to recognition of the role of the Church in the work of peace-making, than to any acknowledgement of our role personally in the Church. But for that recognition to take place, the Church has to be seen as being deeply concerned with the problems of the afflicted, the needs of the deprived, the relief of distress. It may take many different forms which will vary with local social problems. It is only when Christ's concern is apparent to those in need, in the actual issues which confront them, that they will turn to the Church as a reconciler. In the words of Isaiah, as a 'breach-mender'.

For those who live in inner-cities or in the other areas of urban deprivation, there is ground for fresh hope in the promise contained in this text, that 'your ancient ruins will be rebuilt'. The breach-mender is suitably called 'restorer of streets to be lived in'. In the Vauxhall area, near the riverside, in the centre of Liverpool, the work of a co-operative housing association has rightly attracted much attention recently. The local community, which suffered greatly from widespread unemployment, poor housing and lack of job opportunity, came together to establish what is called the Eldonian Village. It is built on the site of the former Tate and Lyle factory, where many local people and their families before them worked. Somehow with great determination they have stayed together, and the way in which they have worked together to secure really pleasant and worthy housing is a noteworthy achievement. Their slogan has been 'We did it better together'. They celebrate the partnership which they have experienced with government agencies and voluntary bodies, and with Churches co-operating in an area where once they feuded.

Not content with this they have taken over an adjoining derelict plot of land, lying immediately over a tunnel, with airvents standing like small brick sentry boxes at regular intervals across the site. The site itself has been given over to the establishment of a market garden, where plants are grown, bedded, developed and ultimately sold. To see this enterprise in the middle of a reclaimed urban development is to recognize a watered garden, symbol of the new life springing up where 'age-old foundations' are just beneath the surface: grace building on nature.

O God of love and compassion,
grant prosperity to your people.
Give faith and initiative
to those who feel deprived and frustrated.
Grant new purpose to the downhearted
and direct the skill of all those
who seek to build for your glory. Amen.

Introduction: Group material

This book is written first of all for personal daily use and we hope that it will be helpful to individuals in their Lenten journey of prayer and reflection. It is also offered to small groups of Christians who wish to travel through Lent together, sharing experience, faith and prayer. Such groups may be newly formed for this purpose or well-established over some time. To assist such small groups – and any parishes or congregations who wish to use it for a Lent programme – there are some suggestions for discussion, reflection and prayer at the end of each week.

These suggestions are offered simply to assist reflection and should be used and adapted according to the needs of the group. It is obviously not important to get through all the points but rather to find a focus for sharing and prayer together. One question from each section may be sufficient. They follow a simple pattern:

Starting points

Questions to help the group settle down.

These will be especially useful to newly formed groups.

Allow 10–15 minutes for these.

Deeper reflection

Questions to help the group to explore the journey of Lent more deeply. The questions invite sharing of faith based on two or three key themes from the readings and reflections of each week.

Give around 45–50 minutes to these questions.

Prayer

A suggestion for a prayer activity to close the meeting.

Allow around 10 minutes.

Group material

Starting points

- What are your hopes for yourself during Lent this year?
- What feelings and thoughts does Ash Wednesday awake in you?
- What aspects of your life need the challenge of Lent?

Deeper reflection

1. Already the Lent Readings have presented a dual challenge:
   - the call to heart-felt repentance.
   - the call to action for social justice.
   - Which aspects of this challenge do you find most difficult?
2. 'You will be called "Breach-mender"' Isaiah 58:12 (Saturday).
   - Are there situations in your life that need a 'breach-mender'?
3. Where, in our society or in your own neighbourhood, do you see most need for Christians to be mending breaches or reconciling conflict?
4. How could your Lent commitment extent to some action of this kind?

Prayer

Recall the Introduction to the book and its description of the wilderness and the vineyard.

Picture in turn first a wilderness and then a vineyard full of workers.

- In which are you most at home?
- When has your life been like a wilderness?
- When has it been like a busy vineyard?

Recall these times and thank the Lord for them.

Say together the prayer from Saturday.

FIRST WEEK OF LENT

'What we are doing is to call both oppressor and oppressed, rich and poor, both blacks and whites, to repentance and in line with the ideals of the Kingdom to take sides with justice and against injustice.'

Frank Chikane
in *'No Life of My Own'*
Page 30

Children in Crossroads, a township outside Cape Town, South Africa, during our visit in May 1989.

First Sunday of Lent
(Matthew 4:1–11)

Then Jesus was led by the Spirit out into the desert to be put to the test by the devil. He fasted for forty days and forty nights, after which he was hungry, and the tester came and said to him, 'If you are Son of God, tell these stones to turn into loaves.' But he replied, 'Scripture says: "Human beings live not on bread alone but on every word that comes from the mouth of God".' The devil then took him to the holy city and set him on the parapet of the Temple. 'If you are Son of God,' he said, 'throw yourself down; for scripture says: "He has given his angels orders about you", and "they will carry you in their arms in case you trip over a stone".' Jesus said to him, 'Scripture also says: "Do not put the Lord your God to the test".' Next, taking him to a very high mountain, the devil showed him all the kingdoms of the world and their splendour. And he said to him, 'I will give you all these, if you fall at my feet and do me homage.' Then Jesus replied, 'Away with you, Satan! For scripture says: "The Lord your God is the one to whom you must do homage, him alone you must serve".' Then the devil left him, and suddenly angels appeared and looked after him.

Matthew 4:1–11

In both St Matthew's gospel and in that of St Luke, the story of the temptations in the wilderness follows immediately on the account of the baptism of Jesus in the Jordan by John the Baptist. None of us can claim to know just how and precisely when Jesus, in his human nature, came to recognize his role in life and the mission entrusted to him by the Father. But his baptism must have been an important moment for him in his dawning awareness. As he came up from the waters of the Jordan, 'suddenly the heavens opened and he saw the Spirit of God descending like a dove and coming down on him. And suddenly there was a voice from heaven, "This is my Son, the Beloved; my favour rests on him"' (Matthew 3:16–17).

These words must have added greatly to his awareness of the Father's calling and his empowerment for his task. What more natural than that Jesus was led by the Spirit into the wilderness. He needed to reflect and pray about his mission, and about how he was to carry it out. His mind must have linked those words spoken as he came out of the Jordan with what he would have known from the prophets, and especially with what we know as the first of the Songs of the Servant: 'Here is my servant whom I uphold, my chosen one in whom my soul delights' (Isaiah 42:1).

If he was to reflect on the manner in which his Messianic mission was to take place, it would almost have prepared him for the form the temptations were to take. The servant of the Lord 'does not cry out or raise his voice ... he does not break the crushed reed or snuff the faltering wick'. There was no doubt about the submission which would be required of him: 'I have offered my back to those who struck me ... I have turned my face away from insult and spitting' (Isaiah 50:6).

Jesus was led by the Spirit out into the wilderness to be tempted by the devil. The whole episode echoes the spiritual journey of the Hebrew people towards the promised land. Their journey was difficult. Jesus also experiences the desert before making those decisions which were to be an indication of the manner in which his redemptive mission was to be achieved. He rejects the worldly standards set before him by stressing his reliance upon the word of God. Each of the three temptations is rebutted out of God's word.

It seems clear from the gospel that he is being tempted to put self-interest before the mission given to him. First, he is tempted to use his power for his own benefit. He has fasted for forty days and nights, so there is the obvious temptation to use his power to provide food for the relief of his hunger. Then he is tempted to use that power for the miraculous protection of himself, by stepping off the high parapet of the temple and counting upon the angels to break what would have been a fatal fall. That would have been a real show of his power. Then, finally, he is tempted to accept dominion over all the kingdoms of the world, provided he would compromise by offering obeisance and homage to a power other than that of his Father. But he will obey and worship and serve the Father, and him alone.

It is significant that the moment Jesus attends to his mission of winning the world back to God, he is subjected to these severe temptations. He is confronted by the reality of evil. Christians have different ideas about the presence of Satan in their lives today. Some have a powerful sense of a personal devil, Satan. Some seem to take over the belief of other faiths, with one good God and another one evil. Yet we believe firmly in one God alone. Many see temptation as St James describes it, being attracted and seduced by one's own wrong desire. However we describe it, there remains the mystery of evil, seducing individuals, infecting whole groups, even nations. Some recognize principalities and powers in the form of organized evil embedded deeply in the structure of society.

When people do not wish to be involved in opposition to evil forces in society today, it is usually due to their falling victim to the temptation to self-interest, personal profit and power. In his autobiography *No Life of My Own*, Frank Chikane, General Secretary of the South African Council of Churches, writes: 'The West, or the business community, tend to support even tyrannical regimes, particularly in the Third World, provided they maintain the necessary stability for them to continue to make their profit, and ensure the so-called national security interests of the rich and powerful nations . . . What we are doing is to call both oppressor and oppressed, rich and poor, both blacks and whites, to repentance and in line with the ideals of the Kingdom to take sides with justice and against injustice'.

Our Lenten journey is likely to be beset with temptations of various kinds. But if we make that journey faithfully, we shall discover not only what kind of Saviour Jesus is for us, but also who we are and where we stand. The temptation is likely to be the extent to which we are prepared to compromise and conform with the world. Our true purpose must be repentance, conversion and renewal. As we journey with Christ in the wilderness, we seek to name evil for what it is and to renew the clear vision of God and his purposes.

Lord God,
guide us on our Lenten journey,
that we may recognize and resist all temptation
to put self-interest before your truth.
For you are the way
and there is no other approach to your Kingdom.
We make this prayer in Jesus' name. Amen.

Monday in First Week of Lent
(Matthew 25:31–46)

'When the Son of man comes in his glory, escorted by all the angels, then he will take his seat on his throne of glory. All nations will be assembled before him and he will separate people one from another as the shepherd separates sheep from goats. He will place the sheep on his right hand and the goats on his left. Then the King will say to those on his right hand, "Come, you whom my Father has blessed, take as your heritage the kingdom prepared for you since the foundation of the world" . . . Then he will say to those on his left hand, "Go away from me, with your curse upon you, to the eternal fire prepared for the devil and his angels" . . .'

Matthew 25:31–34, 41

Today's Reading has generally been taken to refer to the Day of Judgement at the end of time. The criterion for entry into the Kingdom is represented as 'you, whom my Father has blessed'. Is it just something which has been done to us? Is nothing more required of us? In what does the Father's blessing consist which will give us entry into the Kingdom? Christ's new command to his disciples has been 'as I have loved you, so also you ought to love one another'. The Father's blessing must surely be the gift of life and the knowledge, example and love of Christ. When Christ comes again in glory, his judgement will rest upon whether that example has been followed in a loving and serving relationship with others. All will be rewarded or punished in accord with the kindness and compassion they have shown to their neighbour.

This passage from the gospel follows upon the various parables which Jesus has used to stress the need to be vigilant against the Day of Judgement. In the traditional pastoral setting, our Lord speaks easily of the shepherd and his sheep. The manner in which a flock is brought together and checked provides a ready basis for his treatment of the day of reckoning.

Large flocks of sheep run free over moors and through glens: each year they are gathered in. Sturdy sheep-pens make it possible to divide the sheep amidst all the bumping and boring that goes on. It is not difficult for us, amidst all the hurly-burly of our lives, to picture ourselves as part of this annual gathering or calling-in. But it is with the reckoning that we are especially concerned.

At that point the basis of the check-over is made personal, individual, almost 'yes' or 'no'. There can be no evasion nor room for deceit. The judge knows not only all the evidence of the case, but also the motivation, reasoning, weakness or generosity which lay behind the action. The verdict is clear: 'I was hungry; you did/did not give me food. I was thirsty; you did/did not give me drink. I was a stranger; you did/did not make me welcome. I was naked; you did/did not clothe me. I was ill; you did/did not come to see me. I was in prison; you did/did not come to visit me.'

Individually we can today most profitably use the gospel questions for our own examination of conscience, though the charge-list set out in the gospel is not exclusive. But we are also members of society and the gospel tells of 'all nations' being assembled for the judgement. Nowadays we speak sometimes of social sin, by which we mean that we cannot excuse ourselves of our share of guilt for action taken or not taken in our name by our own country, government or community. This can be especially true of sins of neglect or omission. Are we justified in pleading that we did not do anything because we did not know the full story, or because we did not believe that there was any effective action we could take?

How does all this translate into our own lives? As a nation at least we know that there are Third World countries where our neighbours are hungry and perhaps sick from famine or drought. We do not have to look far to come across those who are quite genuinely homeless. There are those with AIDS. The numbers of the unemployed are still immense. And what kind of support are we providing for the separated and the divorced? The great temptation today is to blame people for their own situation, on the pretext that they are shiftless and ne'er-do-wells. We have to recognize our own responsibilities in situations of this kind. Sometimes it is easier if we make a positive effort to recognize the person of Christ himself in those whose needs are evident before us.

Many of us who live in 'comfortable Britain' believe that all our fellow citizens are equally well-off. There can be hidden poverty in some smart areas, if we have eyes to see, and where we can recognize the plight of elderly people, too proud to ask for help and praying that perhaps someone will notice and come to their aid. There are of course many needy people we shall never know, until we bump into them in the sheep-pens on the Day of Judgement. True, we shall find ourselves in close company with people we have known on earth. We may also quickly come to realize that the King and Judge is welcoming some with whom in the past we have been embarrassed to be associated. Perhaps they will include the ones who have been dismissed by our own friends as extremist, unrealistic, left-wing, or obsessive about the poor.

In refusing to support such people, is this where we have failed to give Christ food and drink? How could we have helped? Would there have been any point in giving money to charities engaged in front-line relief work? Those works we do support, do they bring relief to the poor and needy? The list of the top 50 charities in Britain include 40 with no connection with the poor. Do we need to examine our charitable-giving to relief and development agencies?

There will be many surprises, as we bump into one another in the sheep-pens of Judgement Day. We may find some who are welcomed by the King in spite of their having little *personal* contact with the poor. 'Lord, when did we help you?' One person may have done it by insisting in the Board Room that investment should be renewed in an area of high unemployment. Another may have persevered in his Bank on the question of the international debt of poor nations. Another may have challenged regularly the received wisdom of his business colleagues about employment practices. Or perhaps our failing lay in not standing up to an employer who recently told Employment Training officials: 'We'll accept your trainees provided you don't send us any black people'. In the check-over in the sheep-pens of the Kingdom, will we hear those words: 'In so far as you neglected to do this to one of the least of these brothers of mine, you neglected to do it to me'?

Almighty and loving Father, God of Justice,
give us eyes to notice people's needs
and to persevere in seeking ways to meet them.
Forgive us the times we have neglected
these brothers and sisters of Jesus. Amen.

Tuesday in First Week of Lent
(Matthew 6:7–15)

Jesus said to his disciples: 'In your prayers do not babble as the gentiles do,
for they think that by using many words they will make themselves heard.
Do not be like them; your Father knows what you need before you ask him.
So you should pray like this:

Our Father in heaven,
may your name be held holy,
your kingdom come,
your will be done,
on earth as in heaven.
Give us today our daily bread.
And forgive us our debts,
as we have forgiven those who are in debt to us.
And do not put us to the test,
but save us from the Evil One.

'Yes, if you forgive others their failings, your heavenly Father will forgive
you yours; but if you do not forgive others, your Father will not forgive your
failings either.'

Matthew 6:7–15

Several of the Scripture Readings, set before us in the next few weeks, centre on God our Father. At the heart of Jesus' own life were the moments when he withdrew from the crowds in order to be alone with his Father. No less important to him was the powerful motivation he experienced, when he faced busy demands or bitter opposition, to do his Father's will and to finish his work. He wants us to enter into that same experience of knowing God as our Father. So the prayer he teaches us starts in that way: 'Our Father'.

Of course people's experiences will vary as to what 'Father' means in practice. Some fathers provide a model of reliability and love. Others, alas, may have left their children with a picture only of weakness or selfishness. What kind of fatherhood does our Lord point to? In today's reading, the words which follow immediately on the text of the Lord's Prayer, stress the importance to God of forgiveness. When we forgive others, we reflect the character of our heavenly Father. If we fail to do this, and do not forgive others, then we shall find ourselves out of step with him.

The story which points up this characteristic in God's nature most strongly and clearly is the parable of the Prodigal Son (in Luke 15). It is well known, though sometimes it is seen as the parable of the Two Brothers, or even of the Waiting Father. We shall be reading it in these Lent studies a little later on. It has an easy application in life and relationships today, though not everyone accepts what it seems to say. We both served for a time in the East End of London. There we often found that people did not agree with the lesson of the parable. 'If you go on forgiving like that', we were sometimes told, 'the people you try to forgive just spit in your face. Our sympathy goes out to those hard-working elder brothers, who carried the burden of the day when the prodigal was kicking over the traces.'

As church leaders we have sometimes been harangued by journalists and politicians who have said that we should do more condemning of laziness, hooliganism, car-theft and so on, and that we should give more time to teaching standards of morality and a positive approach to discipline. We both would be very happy to present challenges of that kind, though we would rather speak of personal responsibility and self-discipline. But the real point is that condemning and lecturing will not bring about the change of heart in others that is needed. Just what sort of response would such moralizing have upon the young people in a perimeter estate in Merseyside, who recently said, 'Nobody listens to us, so we won't bother talking'?

The way of the Waiting Father is much more costly than delivering ourselves of an easy lecture. His way includes listening to young people who feel alienated and ignored, taking time with them, until they begin to feel that perhaps after all they are valued. It is then that it becomes possible to start talking to them about self-discipline and responsibility.

In the parable the elder son, like some of our East End friends, objects to the weakness and, as he sees things, the unfairness of all this forgiving on the Father's part. The Father himself is hurt by that reaction and attitude which are foreign to his home, and especially by his elder son's self-righteous condemnation and refusal even to acknowledge 'this son of yours' as his own brother. The Father stands his ground: his generosity and graciousness are tough. He will not give way before those harsh and punitive attitudes.

We too have to stand our ground against some of the criticisms of the Church. Archbishop Robert Runcie spoke of this in his enthronement sermon in Canterbury Cathedral in 1980: 'The cry is "The Church must give a firm lead". Yes, it must – a firm lead against rigid thinking, a judging temper of mind, a disposition to oversimplify the difficult and complex problems . . . The throne of Jesus is a mercy-seat. It stands firm against all the vileness of the world, but also for compassion.'

Knowing God as our Father includes bringing him our most personal and intimate needs and longings. Each of us as individuals can think of God as 'my Father'. But the Lord's prayer starts with 'Our Father'. It is all too easy to allow our thoughts and prayers to be limited to the well-being of those who are like-minded with us in worship and belief. Thank God, the Lord's Prayer does not belong to any one Christian denomination. It is his gift to all of us and shared by all of us. To pray 'Our Father' helps to remind us that we belong to the whole people of God. It is our experience that we are enriched when we open ourselves to receive from others the insights which they are able to bring.

Lord, you have taught us to call you 'Father':
thank you that you forgive us again and again.
Help us to forgive those who have wronged us,
and to be numbered amongst those of a generous spirit
who seek to bind your family closer together.
We ask this for the sake of Jesus Christ, your Son, our Lord. Amen.

Wednesday in First Week of Lent
(Luke 11:29–32)

The crowds got even bigger and Jesus addressed them, 'This is an evil generation; it is asking for a sign. The only sign it will be given is the sign of Jonah. For just as Jonah became a sign to the people of Nineveh, so will the Son of man be a sign to this generation. On Judgement Day the Queen of the South will stand up against the people of this generation and be their condemnation, because she came from the ends of the earth to hear the wisdom of Solomon; and, look, there is something greater than Solomon here.

On Judgement Day the men of Nineveh will appear against this generation and be its condemnation, because when Jonah preached they repented; and, look, there is something greater than Jonah here.'

Luke 11:29–32

In the wilderness Jesus had already faced the temptation to win people over by signs which would astonish them. As we saw last Sunday, the idea which the devil planted in the mind of Jesus was to throw himself off the parapet of the Temple, in front of the crowd there, and prove that he came from God by landing safely. His answer was, 'You must not put the Lord your God to the test'. His way was to be the way of costly obedience to his Father's will. There were to be no short cuts, no tricks to prove to people that they must believe in him. For his Father's way was by truth and love to win the hearts and minds of people.

Mark's account of Jesus being asked for a sign is briefer than those given by Matthew and Luke. Some Pharisees engaged him in discussion: to test him, they asked him for a sign from heaven. He sighed deeply to himself and said, 'Why does this generation ask for a sign? I tell you this: no sign shall be given to this generation.' Matthew's account includes a reference to the sign of Jonah: perhaps Matthew has added something in light of knowledge gained after the Resurrection. He includes reference to how Jonah was in the sea monster's belly for three days and three nights, paralleled by the Son of Man being buried for three days before Easter came.

Jesus' deep sigh at their craving for a sign is echoed in his story of the rich man and the poor man at his gate, Divēs and Lazarus: 'If they will not believe Moses and the prophets, neither will they believe if one were to rise from the dead.'

The point of the story, as we have it in today's reading from Luke, is to do with repentance. They had Jesus in their midst, someone greater than Jonah: they knew in their consciences that they should respond to his call to repentance, as the people of Nineveh had done when Jonah preached. That generation had responded to God's truth; this generation kept changing the subject, away from the awkward one of personal and national repentance. If only he would give them a sign, then they would become his followers.

Many people in our generation are fascinated by religion. If the Sunday newspapers understand one thing about what their readers want to read, it is the more curious and astonishing experiences claimed by religious people. To think of religion as a phenomenon is a way of keeping God at arm's length. Like all clergy, we have seen people change the subject from what they have found to be an awkward probing of conscience, to questions about miracles or arguments about what the Church is or is not doing.

The craving for a sign often turns out to be offering to do a deal with God. 'Prove yourself to me, and I will follow you.' 'Heal my child and I will be whole-hearted in my church-going and give large sums to charity.' We are always doing deals with God, demanding health and prosperity from him in return for our prayers and discipleship. The difficulty is the fact that we often forget our part of the bargain when a few months have gone by, perhaps after our child has got well.

With Christ in the wilderness we realize that this approach of doing deals, of performing signs in return for loyal worship, is absolutely foreign to his way. It is one of the devil's ideas which Jesus rejected. His Father's way, our Father's way, is of calling us to enter into a trusting relationship: as we search and find his generosity, his self-emptying and his accepting love, we learn to receive his grace and to respond in love and obedience.

Searching and finding is not only a matter of argument: God certainly wants us to use our minds, but underneath the argument is also a question of using our wills. In St John's gospel, Jesus says, 'Anyone who is prepared to do God's will, will know whether my teaching is from God'.

'I envy you your faith', a man said to a clergyman whose approach was sometimes robust. 'Do you?' he replied; 'then take out your diary and we will make three dates when I will meet you for an hour, and we can get down to some hard thinking about the basis of faith.' The challenge was not accepted. This is an issue of whether we really want to find God's will, and whether we are prepared to do it. We need to be persuaded of where the way of truth and goodness leads.

Repentance is a *religious* word. It involves a change of heart and a turning round towards God. It is as true of us as it was of Jesus' own generation, that we have the possibility of knowing more than the Queen of the South who came searching, and more than the people of Nineveh who repented. If we know about Jesus Christ, we know something greater than Solomon or Jonah. Part of the trouble in countries like Britain is that people assume that they have long known what Christianity is all about. This may be because they have gone to a church school or sung in a church choir. They regard the good news of Jesus Christ as stale and old information; they believe that everyone in Britain understands what the claims of the gospel are.

Repentance is a *personal* word. When the penny drops and people sense that God is addressing them personally, they often say that no one ever told them what the gospel was about before. Later they realize that they did in fact hear much of it before, but somehow their minds were closed. Repentance can also be a *national* word. The people of Nineveh believed what Jonah had to say, proclaimed a fast and put on sackcloth, from the greatest to the least.

In these daily studies we are trying to write about the challenge facing each of us to exercise personal responsibility, self-discipline and care for people close to us. We are also trying to write about the challenge made to us to care for weaker groups, to pursue excellence, and not to be concerned only with the prosperity of our own family or with our sectional interests. We believe that heartfelt repentance is both needed and possible for the people of our generation.

Lord, the good news is within our reach.
Forgive us for the times
when, by closed mind or false religious argument,
we have kept you at arm's length.
Show us your truth and your way,
and strengthen our will to follow.
We ask it that your glory and your love
may be known in our generation. Amen.

Thursday in First Week of Lent
(Matthew 7:7–12)

Jesus said to his disciples: 'Ask, and it will be given to you; search, and you will find; knock, and the door will be opened to you. Everyone who asks receives; everyone who searches finds; everyone who knocks will have the door opened. Is there anyone among you who would hand his son a stone when he asked for bread? Or would hand him a snake when he asked for a fish? If you, then, evil as you are, know how to give your children what is good, how much more will your Father in heaven give good things to those who ask him!

'So always treat others as you would like them to treat you; that is the Law and the Prophets.'

Matthew 7:7–12

Today's gospel Reading comes from the Sermon on the Mount, from which also our extract last Tuesday was taken. St Matthew records the words of the Lord's Prayer and then, after a brief reference to fasting and the need for us to trust the one we can call 'Father', Jesus returns to the subject of effective prayer.

Sad to say, for many people nowadays the word 'Father' does not point in the direction of God at all. Far from it. It emerges that they have suffered lasting emotional hurts which seem to rule out that loving relationship which is intended. It may be that their father opted out of his responsibilities through weakness, by desertion or just neglect through over-busyness. Worse still are those tragic cases of child abuse, much publicized of late. All of us have some fear of being deserted or abandoned, especially when we are growing up. Those who have had the tragic experience of discovering that they could not rely of their own father, sometimes find it quite hard to risk putting their trust in anyone else: even in God.

Yet our Lord often draws on the experience of human parents. Somehow we all know that when parents cannot be relied on, one of the basic foundations of creation is being undermined. We, 'who are evil' says the Lord, still know how to give our children what is good: how much more will our Father in heaven give good things to those who ask him! Not that the mother's role is overlooked. All that parental love can provide is stressed. Through the voice of Isaiah, we hear: 'As a mother comforts her child, so shall I comfort you' (Isaiah 66:13). In a few days' time we will write of that other beautiful passage from the same prophet: 'Can a woman forget her baby at the breast, feel no pity for the child she has borne? Even if these were to forget, I shall not forget you' (Isaiah 49:15). In the life of Jesus here on earth, we find the example of the faithful and supporting love of Mary, his mother. She was utterly and always reliable.

All this is a reminder to us that our heavenly Father is eternally and utterly reliable. So, we are urged, ask, search, knock. The one who asks always receives. The one who searches always finds. Those who knock always have the door opened to them. Always? It would be foolish to deny the voices which also reach us: 'But he did not answer *my* prayer', 'My daughter, who has always worked for other people, is now desperately ill with cancer'; 'Why do the innocent suffer and the ungodly flourish?'

The Psalms – and still more the Book of Job – are full of these complaints to God. They are an encouragement to us to pour out our hearts in prayer, as we would to the most perfect human mother or father we could imagine. Sometimes it will be, if you like, a prayer of protest, including doubt, anger and puzzlement. The Psalmists wrote out of their first-hand experience, in a world where violent oppression and meaningless tragedy caused people to challenge the orthodox wisdom that the righteous always triumph and the wicked bite the dust. In their prayers of protest, the

Psalmists tell God with honesty and pain what they are facing and what are their feelings; and they wrestle with God in order to make sense of it, and to move on beyond it. The Psalms offer us a way not only to articulate our feelings, but also to transform them.

There are no smooth words or easy cure-all answers to the mysteries of suffering and evil. Some would try to claim that God sends suffering. If that were so, we should provide no remedies, not even a hot water bottle to take away the pain. Some say that God gives the victory to those who trust him. In the end, we believe that to be true in the promise of the resurrection of the body; but for many the fruits of victory are not yet. Often our present comfort and reassurance can only be found in our trust in God's all-providing and eternal love.

We have much to learn from the accounts in the gospels of how Jesus reacts with indignation at the presence of evil and suffering. They are intrusions into God's good world. He heals many. He encourages us to tackle suffering by every means: by prayer, scientific discoveries, devoted medical care. Most of all, he enters the darkest tunnel of human suffering, as we shall see on Good Friday. 'My God, my God, why have you forsaken me?' Yet his Father's love remains utterly reliable. Easter Day follows. The Father suffered with him, and suffers with us.

We, members of the Christian company, need to offer each other that same reliable support which we would like others to offer to us. After the terrible football tragedy at Hillsborough in April 1989, there was marvellous response in many of the families and neighbourhoods of our city. People were prepared to sit and listen, as the terrible experiences of that day were repeated over and over again. Many learned that it was not unmanly to weep and to pour out their hurt and their anger, and to seek out a counsellor or a clergyman to help them to look at their deeper fears.

Finding a dependable friend to whom to turn has helped many to discover the reliability of God our Father. We learn not so much to demand 'pennies from heaven', as to find his hand holding ours as we face suffering.

Father, you feel with us the hurts of this world.
We thank you that your loving hand holds us securely, always.
Help us to join in your work of healing,
with our hands, our listening and our prayers.
For Jesus' sake. Amen.

Friday in First Week of Lent

(Ezekiel 18:21–28)

Thus says the Lord: 'If the wicked, however, renounces all the sins he has committed, respects my laws and is law-abiding and upright, he will most certainly live; he will not die. None of the crimes he committed will be remembered against him from then on; he will most certainly live because of his upright actions. Would I take pleasure in the death of the wicked – declares the Lord Yahweh – and not prefer to see him renounce his wickedness and live?'

Ezekiel 18:21–23

This eighteenth chapter of the Book of Ezekiel places fresh emphasis on individual responsibility in Old Testament teaching. Earlier Scriptures were concerned with the individual mainly as part of a family, tribe or nation. Now, some six hundred years before Christ, most of the people of Israel had been taken away into exile in Babylon. Ezekiel was among them. Like the other prophets, he spells out the sins of the nation which had brought down upon them the judgement of God.

They sat down by the waters of Babylon and wept. They had lost prosperity, freedom, Jerusalem, the temple of God. And they knew that they had deserved it. In their gloom they kept repeating an old proverb: 'The parents have eaten unripe grapes; and the children's teeth are set on edge' (Ezekiel 18:2). They had no hope for the future of their children. They saw them simply as the victims of history, written by their parents, and of their environment.

In this gloomy context of national disaster, judgement, defeat and exile, Ezekiel's message is about God's pleasure in the repentance of each individual. For our part, as we read these words, we are reminded of our Lord's parable about the lost sheep: 'There is more rejoicing in heaven over one sinner repenting than over ninety-nine upright people who have no need of repenting' (Luke 15:7).

These Old Testament and New Testament texts insist that, against the odds, repentance is possible for every individual, whatever his background or circumstances. In today's society, and even in the Church today, we are often very unbelieving about the possibility of this. For example, we are all making plans for a great spiritual drive during the next ten years, whether we call it a Decade of Evangelism or a Decade of Evangelization. It is due to begin at Christmas 1990 and to last until the turn of the century. Clearly it is a time calling for real commitment from Christians; but it is worth pausing to ask ourselves what we really expect can be achieved during this period leading up to the year 2000.

We must of course hope that, with renewed enthusiasm amongst the people of God, many who have lapsed from childhood faith may return; and we can hope that many more who are on the fringe of the Christian community may make up their minds to get off the fence and commit themselves as whole-hearted followers of our Lord Jesus Christ. That would be very good news indeed. But there must be a real fear lest in many a parish, as its people think in advance about its plans, there will be a number who will write off any possibility of new Christians emerging from 'that troublesome group of teenagers', or from that 'hard to let' estate – or should we more honestly call it that 'hard to live in' estate?

For years people have refused housing in such estates because their reputation has been that 'they only put problem families there'. It was of a place regarded in this way that it was said, 'Nazareth? Can anything good come from that place?' Jesus came from Nazareth. There is no area, no district or environment, from which he is unable to call forth the repentance of an individual, bringing rejoicing in heaven. In our plans for the next decade, we hope that parishes which include such 'hard to let' estates, will make determined and patient approaches to people living there, to help them to feel able to say, 'This Christ could be for me too'.

Today's Scripture makes it clear that every individual is responsible before God for his own life, whatever his or her background. That does not mean that God expects exactly the same achievement, in kind or degree, from each individual. We have different starting points, different possibilities. Our Lord recognized this: 'When someone is given a great deal, a great deal will be demanded of that person; when someone is entrusted with a great deal, of that person even more will be expected' (Luke 12:48). He speaks also of the person who is given less and of the fact that less is therefore expected of him. But nowhere is there the suggestion that to some nothing is given, and of them nothing is expected.

There can be no justification for treating individuals as statistics, for regarding human beings as 'cases' – 'poor things', who need to have things done for them. Treating people with respect includes expecting them to take personal responsibility for what is within the bounds of possibility for them. But that does not let off the hook those to whom a great deal has been given. As individuals we play a part in society, with responsibility to change the course of events so that people are no longer required to make their homes in such 'hard to live in' estates, as we have mentioned.

However long we have walked with Christ, Ezekiel's challenge to face our individual responsibilities may pull us up sharply this week. It may mean a number of different stands being taken by various persons: questioning and even refusing to go along with company policy, with assumptions of other members of the club or organization to which we belong, or with prejudices of members of our own family. The question put by the Lord to Ezekiel was: 'If the upright abandons uprightness and does wrong by copying all the loathsome practices of the wicked, is he to live?' (Ezekiel 18:24).

Lord, you loved the world so much
that you gave your only Son;
and we, your people, have this good news to share.
Inspire us to believe in the possibility of repentance
both in ourselves and in those who seem furthest from you.
Make us more the kind of Church
in which they may expect to find good news.
We ask this through Christ our Lord. Amen.

Saturday in First Week of Lent
(Matthew 5:43–48)

Jesus said to his disciples: 'You have heard how it was said, "You will love your neighbour" and hate your enemy. But I say this to you, love your enemies and pray for those who persecute you; so that you may be children of your Father in heaven, for he causes his sun to rise on the bad as well as the good, and sends down rain to fall on the upright and the wicked alike. For if you love those who love you, what reward will you get? Do not even the tax collectors do as much? And if you save your greetings for your brothers, are you doing anything exceptional? Do not even the gentiles do as much? You must therefore set no bounds to your love, just as your heavenly Father sets none to his.'

Matthew 5:43–48

Back again to St Matthew and his account of the Sermon on the Mount. Here we find Jesus taking the strong moral base of the commandments of the Jewish Law (the *Torah*), and moving on from it to deal with motives and with strongly held attitudes towards others, especially those outside the local or tribal community to which an individual might belong. Love your neighbour, hate your enemy, was the code for someone accepting strong obligations within the traditional limits of the Law. Jesus said, you must set no bounds to your love, even when it comes to your enemies. His basis for saying this was not some new code of laws that he was delivering. The gospels are not about another law-giver. Rather, he was asking in effect what kind of God we worship and follow. That led on to his words about our Father in heaven, and his presentation of the Lord's Prayer (which we considered last Tuesday).

As we saw then, when we turn to our Father in prayer, we receive the personal comfort of his forgiveness and the reassurance that comes from his reliability through thick and thin. Now Jesus insists that our prayers and our love cannot stop short at our own needs and those of our own particular circle. We must set no bounds to our love, just as our heavenly Father sets no bounds to his.

Many Christians have come to delight in Dietrich Bonhoeffer's description of Jesus as the *Man for Others*. We perhaps forget how unpopular that aspect of his ministry made him with his own people. They called him the friend of tax-gatherers and sinners. We have been glad that he was called the friend of sinners. We have not always stopped to realize just how despised the tax-gatherers were: how they were regarded as traitors working on behalf of an army of occupation. Correspondingly bitter was the criticism he had to endure, which said he was on *their* side.

His critics also said of him, 'Are we not right in saying that you are a Samaritan and possessed by a devil?' (John 8:48). Jesus seemed to them always to be pointing out when a Samaritan did something good. They believed that they had been brought up rightly to hate Samaritans, their bitter foreign rivals, often likened to renegade Jews. A major cause of contention was when Jesus even made a Samaritan the good hero of a parable. Undoubtedly those of his own people opposed to his teaching resented the fact that Jesus seemed to be showing sympathy with 'the others' – outsiders, bad characters – whereas they would have expected him to devote more time to comforting or encouraging those who were loyally fighting for the purity of the Jewish law.

Experience shows that when we raise the needs of the hungry world, or speak up for ethnic minority groups in our own country, or for opportunities for the 'other' community in Northern Ireland – be it the Roman Catholics or the Protestants – someone is very likely to come back at us with the charge of neglecting in some manner those thought to have a more immediate call upon our attentions. 'Charity begins at home', we are told, with an authority given to those words which would suggest that they come from the Bible. Nowhere in the Bible is that text to be found. It is a saying based on a philosophy stemming from fear that love will only stretch so far, and may be exhausted if we include the 'others' in our concern. Read today's text again. Jesus is saying that tax-collectors and foreigners care for their own circle. Christian morality has not entered into it at that point. It begins when we start to reflect the character of this generous Father of all, who sets no limits to his love.

After the 1981 riots in Toxteth (a district of Liverpool), we found ourselves wedged in very uncomfortably between different groups, both of whom felt their hurts very keenly. One couple very close to us told us of their son, a policeman, scarred for life by a brick in the face. Others, whose long-term involvement in the Inner City we admired greatly, told us that, without condoning the violence, they understood the sense of oppression which many black people felt, and why at last their feelings had boiled over.

How would the Father of all react? How were we to react? When leaders in the black community asked if we would help in establishing a Law Centre in Liverpool 8, after careful consideration we firmly supported the project, which has allowed many people for the first time to see the law as a friend rather than as an apparent oppressor. Some of our suburban parishes and groups passed fierce resolutions, demanding that the Church should only give money to church projects. It was clear to us that the Father, of whom Jesus spoke in those verses from the Sermon on the Mount, set no such limits to his generosity.

> *Heavenly Father,*
> *we are sometimes afraid*
> *of setting no limits to our love.*
> *Take away those fears.*
> *Help us to learn from your generosity*
> *to both the deserving and the undeserving.*
> *We make our prayer through Jesus Christ,*
> *your Son, even the Man for Others. Amen.*

Group material

Starting points

- How are you doing with your Lent resolutions?
- What point struck you most from this week's Readings and commentary?

Deeper reflection

1. The week began with the story of the temptations of Christ in the wilderness and the invitation drawn from that Gospel to all of us to discover who we are and where we stand this Lent.
   - What are the most difficult temptations for Christians in this country in our present social and political situation?
   - What kind of things do you think of as personal temptations?

2. Do we really have social and political matters on our consciences . . . or do we tend to see morality as mainly concerning personal matters?

3. On Monday, reflecting on the story of the last judgement, we spoke of our responsibility towards those who are poor in our world.
   - How far do you feel responsibility for the poor should go?

4. Recall some of the news you have heard or read or seen this week.
   - What has distressed you?
   - Where has there been suffering?

Break into groups of around three, and in each small group write a psalm for today . . . tell God how you are feeling about our world, his world. It could be about one issue or about everything. It might be a psalm of protest, or doubt, or anger or puzzlement or shame. Share your psalms.

Prayer

The challenges from this week's readings are not easy.

The consolation is also present in the equal insistence that our God is a father who waits and listens and whose love makes possible our change of heart.

• Tell the Lord, in prayer, the change of heart that you need during this Lent.

• Ask him to wait and listen. Explain the difficulties.

• Recall his eagerness to accept you, and thank him.

• Say the Our Father together slowly.

SECOND WEEK OF LENT

'Presenting the face of Christ to the world is not a matter of looks, though the expression on the face matters more than the features. But the preacher is not to project himself. It is to the truths of Christ that he calls attention: by word and by example.'

Page 55

Bishop David with
'Christ upon an ass' by Brian Burgess,
Liverpool Parish Church

Second Sunday of Lent
(Matthew 17:1–9)

Six days later, Jesus took with him Peter and James and his brother John and led them up a high mountain by themselves. There in their presence he was transfigured: his face shone like the sun and his clothes became as dazzling as light. And suddenly Moses and Elijah appeared to them; they were talking with him. Then Peter spoke to Jesus. 'Lord,' he said, 'it is wonderful for us to be here; if you want me to, I will make three shelters here, one for you, one for Moses and one for Elijah.' He was still speaking when suddenly a bright cloud covered them with shadow, and suddenly from the cloud there came a voice which said, 'This is my Son, the Beloved; he enjoys my favour. Listen to him.'

Matthew 17:1–5

St Matthew's account of the Transfiguration follows almost at once upon St Peter's confession that Jesus was the Messiah. This had brought forth praise and special recognition from our Lord, but also a warning that his way would be that of the suffering servant, not the path of the triumphant victor. Peter had promptly protested and tried to cut his Master short. When soon afterwards, on the mountain-top, he sees his Lord transfigured, he is only too anxious to prolong this vision of glory. He recognizes the figures on either side of Jesus as the very personification in the Old Testament of the Law and the Prophets. It is their work which his Master is to bring to perfection. No wonder that he exclaims, 'It is good for us to be here'.

Peter seems to have been able to banish from his mind the earlier sombre warnings about suffering. Instead, there is now the heavenly voice speaking of Jesus as the beloved Son of God. He really needs no encouragement to listen to the voice of the one on whose words he has already begun to hang. Here is the definitive teacher. When the cloud lifts and he sees only Jesus, he has no eyes nor need for anyone else. His Lord has not come to destroy the Law and the prophets, but to fulfil them.

The effect of this vision on Peter, James and John, was remarkable. Now there could be no doubt about the authenticity of their Master. In some sense this episode offsets the shock of the temptations of Christ, set out for us a week ago. Stress on Christ's humanity, tempted in the wilderness, is balanced by this revelation of his divinity on the mountain of the Transfiguration. To the disciples it was an affirmation that the firm but humble manner in which he had dealt with the tempter was the way of the Messiah. What they saw and heard served to strengthen their faith and eventually their understanding. But the insight was only momentary. They did not need to be told to listen, so overwhelming was the vision. Later events were to show how frail human memory and faith can be under the pressure of adversity.

What they experienced was for the chosen three disciples a precious privilege. As they go down the mountain, they are told to keep it to themselves. Generally, it is not the way of the Master to reveal to others his divine powers and majestic glory. The return from the clouds means that the disciples will once more witness the firm but humble human stance adopted by their Lord, when tempted to reveal himself in the desert wilderness.

For most of us these days that is the authentic line for the Christian: firm, humble, reliant upon the experience of faith which can be more or less intense, often in relation to the fervour of our life of prayer. A spiritual experience – even allowing for the difference in degree between the disciples' vision of their transfigured Lord, and our passing sense of being close to a loving God – is sometimes unsought and startling. More often it comes as a result of a conscious prayerful placing of oneself 'in the presence of God', as the prayer-books recommend. Whether it brings deep spiritual consolation, such as Peter felt on the mountain-top, undoubtedly depends upon God's gift to those who turn to him. It is part of our human condition that such a deep spiritual experience is passing, probably momentary. Then the bright cloud will lift and we can feel once more the vulnerability of being alone.

'What goes up must come down' is the old saying. It will be true of the stones we may throw into the air. It is also true of the high spots in our life of prayer. There are moments of insight and satisfaction when to pray and be conscious of communication with God is relatively straightforward. There are other dry-as-dust periods which call for almost heroic perseverance. There is no reason to believe that prayer of praise and thanksgiving, carried through in such drear circumstances, is any less pleasing to the Lord.

Our life of faith, our working-life itself, can often be our prayer for the day. It too will have its high spots and its moments of dreary depression, when all around us seems a challenge or contradiction to our faith. To recognize Christ transfigured in his people, in factory and office, in hospital and school, need be no more difficult than to feel his presence in the sanctuary of a quiet and beautiful place of worship. For each of us there is the need to 'listen to him'. The test comes when because of the din about us, we cannot distinguish his words to us. At such a time we prove our love and witness to our faith if we can mean it when we say, 'It is wonderful for us to be here'.

Today we can pray with the Breviary hymn:

Transfigured Christ, believed and loved,
in you our only hope has been:
Grant us, in your unfathomed love,
those things no eye has ever seen.
O Father, Son and Spirit blest,
with hearts transfigured by your grace,
May we your matchless splendour praise
and see the glory of your face. Amen.

Monday in Second Week of Lent
(Luke 6:36–38)

Jesus said to his disciples: 'Be compassionate just as your Father is
compassionate. Do not judge, and you will not be judged; do not condemn,
and you will not be condemned; forgive, and you will be forgiven. Give, and
there will be gifts for you: a full measure, pressed down, shaken together, and
overflowing, will be poured into your lap; because the standard you use will
be the standard used for you.'

Luke 6:36–38

This short extract from our Lord's teaching of his disciples contains three very important points of guidance in the Christian life. We must try to imitate the Father in all things; we cannot pick and choose. We must not condemn or be critical of others in matters where we expect our own failures or weaknesses to be passed over. If we are to forgive and expect to be forgiven, we must ourselves show compassion.

In recent years the word 'compassion' has become a politically sensitive term. It is certainly of major importance at this time, but sadly it has for some figures in public life become identified with being a 'wet'. The dictionary may tell us that it means 'merciful' or 'inclined to be pitying'. The former may fit this gospel passage, but the latter sounds somewhat patronizing. In fact the derivation of the word suggests a common feeling of sympathy, understanding, even of shared suffering.

As a word employed in political rhetoric, it was used some time ago by a well-known Government minister as an indicator of the amount of help given by the State to its citizens. It was something over and above the provision of resources through taxation. Indeed it was something freely disbursed from the surplus achieved by an individual benefitting from tax-relief. Such an abuse of the word fails totally to take into consideration the element of *sharing*, which is at the heart of the meaning of 'compassion'.

Dare we hope to share in the compassion of God? This is where the additional notion of suffering enters in. Our sufferings and sacrifices can be only a pale imitation of the Lord's suffering for our sake. But it is essential to the relationship we must have with others, and it gives meaning and direction to the attitude we adopt towards personal pain. Often it will imply more than just an attitude of mind. Without being patronizing, a compassionate person will often show sensitivity towards the bereaved or someone in distress by trying to share *by presence* the sorrow and stress of the sufferer. This may not be possible. A letter may have to suffice. Normally the shared feelings or sympathy of compassion need to be expressed.

Of course there are times when we feel that someone deserves to be blamed. When we find ourselves taking up the position of judge or withholding forgiveness, we should remember the saying, 'If you point a finger at someone else, four fingers are at the same time pointing back at yourself'. We too deserve judgement. We learn to be compassionate from the way God treats us. On Tuesday of next week we shall read of the man whose master forgave him a vast debt. He promptly went out and had his fellow servant, owing him just a few pounds, thrown into prison until the whole debt was paid.

We have noticed that those who are harsh in their judgement of others, are often harshest of all to themselves. They may say, 'I believe in the forgiveness of sins' but they have not learned to forgive themselves. It is when the wonder of God's undeserved forgiveness for ourselves dawns upon us, that we find we can come easily alongside those who have landed themselves in trouble. We have often used the phrase 'being there' in connection with compassion. It is difficult to be sensitive to the pains and problems of others from a distance.

Attached to a large children's hospital near where we live in Liverpool is a Bereavement Centre. On a recent visit there, we found ourselves in a room with a group of young parents, all of whom had lost a baby in the last few years. 'When our Kenny died on Christmas Eve', a young 'mum' told us, 'I felt that nothing like that had ever happened to anyone before.' She paused. 'It's worse at Christmas. But Father Tom was great. I think he felt worse than I did. You see, Kenny was the first baby he had ever baptised.' We talked for a while about what the books call a 'spiritual relationship', and then she went on. 'And when Kenny got cremated on New Year's Eve,

Father Tom was as bad as the others. That evening he was so upset, he came round to the house and just sat on the floor and played with the other two children. It was great. I'd never realized that priests could care like that.'

The young woman thought for a bit. 'I suppose that it was because Kenny was the first baby Father Tom had baptised.' She looked enquiringly at us, and accepted without difficulty our suggestion that such a situation is always sad and gets no easier for a priest, no matter how long he is at it. 'Every case is one-off and special,' we explained. 'That's right,' she agreed. 'It made such a difference. Father Tom sort of shared Kenny's death with us.'

That young bereaved mother had just explained the true notion of compassion. Nothing condescending about it, but 'suffering with', which is the real meaning of the word. Sitting on the floor, playing with the other children, the young priest had in his own helpless distress been the hands of Christ's compassion outstretched to a family in its grief.

Father in heaven,
you gave your Son Jesus
to suffering and to death on the cross,
and raised him to glory.
Forgive us our forgetfulness and ingratitude.
Help us by our patience and forgiveness
to be a sign of your Son's compassion,
and of faith in times of darkness. Amen.

Tuesday in Second Week of Lent
(Matthew 23:1–12)

Then addressing the crowds and his disciples Jesus said, 'The scribes and the Pharisees occupy the chair of Moses. You must therefore do and observe what they tell you; but do not be guided by what they do, since they do not practise what they preach. They tie up heavy burdens and lay them on people's shoulders, but will they lift a finger to move them? Not they! Everything they do is done to attract attention . . . The greatest amongst you must be your servant. Anyone who raises himself up will be humbled, and anyone who humbles himself will be raised up.'

Matthew 23:1–5, 11–12

Moses' seat is the name of a piece of furniture in the synagogue, from which the preacher delivered the address. As our Lord was addressing the crowds as well as his disciples, his admonition was to congregation and preacher alike: to listen well to words spoken with authority, and for the preacher to avoid pride or hypocrisy in the exercise of his important and, to some extent at least, authoritative role.

It is interesting that to this day, in his address to one presented for ordination to the priesthood, the ordaining bishop is required to remind the candidate to 'meditate on the law of God, believe what you read, teach what you believe, and put into practice what you teach'. Lest that place all emphasis upon formal preaching, the bishop then adds, 'Let the doctrine you teach be true nourishment for the people of God. Let the example of your life attract the followers of Christ, so that by word and action you may build up the house which is God's Church' (*Roman Pontifical*, ICEL Translation).

'Practise what you preach' is an old British proverb, which nowadays applies to anyone in public life and not just to religious ministry. Teachers and parents, responsible for training their children, will also know the importance of example if a lesson is to be learned. 'Hypocrisy' is one of the most detested traits in a character, far outweighing in contempt and criticism most other forms of human weakness. It is the very opposite of what most people mean nowadays when they describe someone as being 'very sincere'. We are prepared to forgive a person like this for honest inadequacy, perhaps especially in the case of a preacher whose character has a greater clarity than his choice of words.

Another curious phenomenon of the present age is the way people claim that they can read the integrity of someone appearing on television. There are of course characters who deliberately foster the image of being a person whom viewers love to hate. But not with the gospel. When the teachings of Christ are to be made known, directly or indirectly, it is the gospel of love and justice and truth which must be preached. 'Word and example' means that the message may be defaced or strengthened by the manner of its presentation, and that is inevitably related to the commitment and integrity of the presenter, the messenger, the preacher.

Presenting the face of Christ to the world is not a matter of looks, though the expression on the face matters more than the features. But the preacher or speaker is not to project himself. It is to the truths of Christ that he calls attention: by word and by example. Practising what you preach is all about that: in the pulpit, the chair of Moses, or the domestic circumstances in which the gospel is to be lived.

In the gospels the scribes and the Pharisees were a frequent target for criticism, because of the gap between their knowledge of the Law and their application of it to the needs of others: the difference between the letter and the spirit of the Law. Fearing that Jesus threatened their position as religious leaders, they used their expertise to prepare trick questions designed to throw him into apparent conflict with the generally accepted obligations of the Law. When elsewhere in the gospel they are denounced as 'whited sepulchres', it is because of the obligations they imposed upon others through their interpretation of the Law which they themselves did not observe.

The criticism laid against them by Jesus in this particular passage is precisely that in their rigorous interpretation of the letter of the Law, they are building up an unnecessary sense of guilt amongst their hearers. What was worse was that it concerned observances to which they paid scant attention themselves. Their unfortunate hearers did not even have the strength of their official and personal example to help them sustain such weight of guilt.

There are preachers today who bind heavy burdens on people: they assume that the godly and hard-working will always be prosperous, and they condemn the weak and disadvantaged in a manner quite unknown in the gospel of the Christ they claim to represent. The abuse is not restricted to the pulpit. It was heartening some years ago to hear a young priest turn upon his television interviewer one evening to protest that it was altogether unfair to hang upon his poor and elderly parishioners responsibility for their poverty and disadvantage.

To criticize the unemployed for their joblessness, to suggest that those without a job must be 'work-shy', and that the presence of a 'black economy' proves that they are all picking up money that way, can be worse than self-righteousness. When charges of this kind are made, they should be challenged in the name of honesty and justice. Silence can be taken as consent.

A few years ago, a leading article in *The Times* claimed that we all knew unemployed people doing well out of the 'informal economy'. A well-known industrialist went further and put a very high figure on those engaged in this practice. We decided that we must challenge this slur on unemployed people. In a letter to the newspaper we questioned whether his figures had any known base and quoted research to show that the profitable parts of the informal economy belonged to those who were in a job, owned a van or their own set of tools, and were 'moonlighting'. The industrialist's charges against the unemployed were unsubstantiated. Our letter was duly printed but there was no come-back. Nevertheless charges of that kind against the disadvantaged always leave some 'mud' behind. The poor and disadvantaged are often the most vulnerable and defenceless targets for hypocritical moralizing and condemnation. For they lack access to the normal means of defence and, if necessary, counter-attack.

Lord, grant us the spirit of knowledge and understanding,
so that, by word and example, we may present your truth
in a manner which speaks of your love and compassion;
and forgive us when our commitment wavers
and our example falls short
of what is asked of us in your name. Amen.

Wednesday in Second Week of Lent
(Matthew 20:17–28)

Then the mother of Zebedee's sons came with her sons to make a request of him, and bowed low; and he said to her, 'What is it you want?' She said to him, 'Promise that these two sons of mine may sit one at your right hand and the other at your left in your kingdom.' Jesus answered, 'You do not know what you are asking. Can you drink the cup that I am going to drink?' They replied, 'We can.' He said to them, 'Very well; you shall drink my cup, but as for seats at my right hand and my left, these are not mine to grant; they belong to those to whom they have been allotted by my Father.'

Matthew 20:20–23

Jesus was on the road to Jerusalem. He had the disciples with him and he warned them of the fate that awaited him. Clearly they had not understood him; perhaps they had not wanted to. But they must have had a mounting sense that the climax of his mission was approaching. Even if he spoke about arrest and death, he spoke also of rising again. That Kingdom of his, after which they hankered, could not be far off. Now was the time to make sure of their own place in it.

It could well be that they were themselves reluctant to mention the matter. But not the mother of the sons of Zebedee. What feminists today would make of that description it is hard to imagine, though later she seems to have been identified with Salome. (At Santiago de Compostela a statue of St Salome stands near the shrine of St James.) At all events she was not bashful about coming forward, certainly not where her sons were concerned. So she asks Jesus for an assurance that her two boys would sit on either side of him in the Kingdom he was shortly to establish.

'Drinking the cup that I drink' means sharing the suffering Christ is to endure. It seems unlikely that the mother, ambitious for her sons' position, will have understood the phrase. It is James and John who reply that they can. Very well, says Jesus, they may drink of his cup, share his suffering; but it is not for him to allocate rewards of such human proportions. That is for his Father, the God of judgement.

Years later it was James, the son of Zebedee, who was the first of the apostles to suffer death for his Master's cause. John the beloved disciple may well have been spared martyrdom but there was no lack of suffering in his long life. But their immediate discomfiture was to be at the hands of the other disciples, who were far from pleased at over-hearing the special pleading of their colleagues' mother. Jesus gives them all a reminder that there is no room amongst his faithful followers for ambition: 'anyone who wants to be great among you must be your servant' (Matthew 20:26).

For some people ambition often proves a strong incentive; but personal ambition amongst friends is usually poison. We may speak about healthy rivalry and nowadays we hear that the competitive spirit produces the best results. But the end can never justify the means. Competition, carried through at the expense of others, can be harmful to all parties, even to the one who at the time may seem to be the winner.

Put in a slightly different way, Christians have some searching questions to ask when they are given the opportunity of holding a position of some power and responsibility. Humility seems to call us to seek the back seat and to avoid any limelight. There are proper warnings about ways in which power can corrupt. Yet when we describe the powerlessness which some people experience, we do not celebrate it: we want to see them given some power to shape their destiny. Keeping our hands clean, avoiding the temptations of power, may mean that we put up with a poor organization or evil circumstances – when perhaps God is calling us to join him in changing the course of events. The way of Christian humility may then mean accepting that God has given us a certain ability and that we must respond to his call.

In being called to be a bishop, each of us likes to speak of authority; but we also acknowledge the dangers of having some power. For us, as for others, power needs to be made accountable; and we try to put ourselves in situations where we are called to account by lay people, clergy, our fellow bishops and church leaders of other Churches.

It is true that some positions of responsibility have to be accepted as a result of obedience. That is why we speak always of the service of authority rather than the exercise of power. Such obedience may well demand a spirit of resignation, but power can corrupt. The greater the responsibility, the more important it is to have a spiritual counsellor, capable of honesty as well as of encouragement and support.

Where it happens to be our responsibility to allocate tasks to others, we have to try to see personal considerations within the setting of the general good. We must bear in mind the family responsibilities of the married person, just as we must measure the greater availability of the celibate against his possible vulnerability under certain circumstances. We must always remember that we are dealing with individuals, even when we are appointing to corporate responsibility; as far as possible, we must try to avoid the advancement of one at the unreasonable hurt or expense of another.

Some years ago a bishop called for volunteers amongst his clergy for a very demanding missionary task far overseas. The most promising candidate was a young priest whose mother had just died. The bishop was concerned about the priest's elderly father who would be left on his own and must be lonely. So the bishop called on the old widower to ask how he would feel if his son was abroad for some years. The reply was immediate: 'You send him where you think he is most needed, Bishop. Then I shall be happy enough.' The answer was worthy of the gospel. The needs of the mission of the Church are often paramount.

Lord Jesus Christ,
forgive us those occasions
when self-seeking and wrong ambition
have damaged the humble generosity
you have asked of your disciples;
and give us the courage
to accept responsibility when you call us,
who came to be the servant of all. Amen.

Thursday in Second Week of Lent

(Jeremiah 17:5–10)

'The heart is more devious than any other thing,
and is depraved; who can pierce its secrets?
I, Yahweh, search the heart,
test the motives,
to give each person what his conduct
and his actions deserve.'
Jeremiah 17:9–10

In our Lenten examination of conscience we become aware both of our weaknesses and of the excuses we like to make for ourselves to diminish our responsibility and the degree of our guilt. Today from Jeremiah we receive the assurance that nothing escapes the knowledge of God. He searches our hearts, knows the measure of our sinfulness and of our more worthy actions, and will punish and reward accordingly. This can be both encouraging and rather frightening. It is as well to recall that in the previous verses the prophet speaks of the trust we may place in Yahweh, and how foolish we are to place all our trust in human beings.

Because it is so close to life itself, the heart is thought of as a place for inner-most feelings and the possession of truth. When Jeremiah speaks of the human heart as being devious, it is as if something held in the heart is so secret that it is not to be betrayed by outward appearances. Who shall know the inner-most thoughts or feelings of another, save the Lord Yahweh who, as the old Catechism reminds us, knows even our most secret thoughts? This he does despite all attempts on our part to disguise the depth of our feelings, to deceive with regard to our motivation and true intention.

That is sharp criticism, harsh judgement, by Jeremiah, tortured by suffering in trying to bring the people of Judah to recognize and renounce their infidelity and false, insincere worship. For so much of the time, Jeremiah claims, they have been in bad faith. Perhaps a sharp reminder of the Lord's total knowledge and understanding of their situation and their motives may help to bring them to their senses. Where Yahweh is concerned, there can be no deceit, no cover-up.

For those of us who are well used to having to explain our motives, the background to our decisions, there can be great comfort from our confidence that the Lord understands our situation fully. There is no need for our excuses where he is concerned. We do not have to ask him to make allowances. That does not mean that all our decisions and judgements are correct.

It is our integrity which comes under examination. The Lord's judgement will be justice itself and, because he is our loving Lord, his will be merciful justice. But if we are to expect his mercy, there must be a heartfelt conversion on our part. That total knowledge, in which we take comfort, means that nothing escapes his attention; nor can we expect him to overlook the manner in which we may foolishly but deliberately have ignored the grace available to us to overcome temptation.

One of the things about which we are most sensitive is when we are criticized or condemned for doing something of which we are quite innocent, and this as a result of false or partial evidence being laid against us. We know how difficult it can be to correct a false report or impression given to others by the grapevine in the office or even by the media. When we feel sorry for ourselves about such a situation, we need to remember not only the many occasions on which false reports circulated about Jesus, the miracle-worker, but also the enormity of his trial and the false witness upon which he was condemned to death. Others have died and continue to die as a result of rigged or distorted evidence. But here was the Son of God, the way, the truth and the life, sentenced to cruel death.

Christ chose to remain silent before his accusers. That is not an easy lesson to learn, nor example to follow. We are all too ready to make excuses for our alleged guilt, or to explain away our own involvement, but in a manner which inevitably implicates someone else. To remain silent under false accusation because to reply can only harm another may seem a counsel of perfection. It can be Christ-like, and is possible only when we have confidence in the Lord who knows how to search our hearts and test our motives.

Today's lesson from Jeremiah is not only about how we hope to be judged ourselves. The boot can be on the other foot. We ourselves must be on our guard lest we rush to rash judgement about others.

A classic case, involving all these elements, took place in London many years ago. Information reached a priest concerning an incident implicating the propriety of a schoolmaster in his parish. The teacher came to see the priest, agreed to the truth of the charges and that he must either resign his post or be suspended pending investigations. The priest advised the teacher to go home and tell his wife, who of course was in ignorance of the whole affair. Instead, the teacher, desperate and feeling unable to face the consequences, drove his car to a remote place and gassed himself with fumes from the exhaust.

When the body was found, all that was known at home by the man's family, and at school by other members of the staff, was that the dead man had had certain worries and had gone to see the priest. No one other than the priest and his original anonymous informant knew the nature of the man's anxieties. The widow and family were of course totally oblivious of the charges laid against the teacher's propriety. They held him in both affection and admiration, and concluded that the priest must have threatened him in some serious way which led to his desperate suicide.

At the coroner's inquest the priest was called to give evidence. He had to choose between revealing the dead man's secret, thereby destroying the widow's image of her husband, and the alternative which was not to defend himself against the charge that his interview with the guilty teacher was so harsh and insensitive as to drive the man to take his life. The priest chose to remain silent and to endure a tongue-lashing from the coroner and subsequently from the widow. He trusted the Lord to ensure that his parishioners would retain sympathetic understanding of their priest.

Years were to pass before a chance meeting between the dead man's son and the original informant put the record straight. By then the widow had followed her unfortunate husband to the Kingdom of mercy and justice.

Lord God, you search the human heart
and know the weakness of our will.
Help us to have faith in your merciful and total understanding
of all the motives which guide us.
May we ourselves avoid hasty and rash judgements
and try always to think the best
of those who treat us unfairly.
We ask this through Christ our Lord. Amen.

Friday in Second Week of Lent
(Matthew 21:33–43, 45–46)

Jesus said to the chief priests and the elders: 'There was a man, a landowner, who planted a vineyard; he fenced it round, dug a winepress in it and built a tower; then he leased it to tenants and went abroad. When vintage time drew near he sent his servants to the tenants to collect his produce. But the tenants seized his servants, thrashed one, killed another and stoned a third. Next he sent some more servants, this time a large number, and they dealt with them in the same way. Finally he sent his son to them thinking, "They will respect my son." But when the tenants saw the son, they said to each other, "This is the heir. Come on, let us kill him and take over his inheritance." So they seized him and threw him out of the vineyard and killed him. Now when the owner of the vineyard comes, what will he do to those tenants?' They answered, 'He will bring those wretches to a wretched end and lease the vineyard to other tenants who will deliver the produce to him at the proper time.' Jesus said to them, 'Have you never read in the scriptures:

The stone which the builders rejected
has become the cornerstone;
this is the Lord's doing
and we marvel at it?

'I tell you, then, that the kingdom of God will be taken from you and given to a people who will produce its fruit.'

When they heard his parables, the chief priests and the scribes realised he was speaking about them, but though they would have liked to arrest him they were afraid of the crowds, who looked on him as a prophet.

Matthew 21:33–46

Back to St Matthew again and a chance to see what religious authority at the time made of our Lord's parables. To teach in parables was not so unusual in the culture of that period. But so often those who heard Christ were ready to apply his words to others rather than put themselves in the picture he was painting in his colourful parables.

Jesus had been in the Temple, teaching. The chief priests and the elders had challenged his authority. He had countered by asking what authority they accorded to John the Baptist. They had quickly backed away for fear lest they arouse the people who plainly held John to be a prophet. In the account given by St Matthew, Jesus followed this up with two fairly pointed parables. This time they decided that the application of these examples must be aimed at themselves. So began the planning and conspiracy which led ultimately to his arrest.

In the verses immediately before the full reading for today, Matthew starts with the parable of the two sons: one who promises to obey his father but does not do so; and the other who is unwilling to commit himself in obedience, but subsequently goes and does what he has been asked. The lesson is reasonably clear: it is the chief priests and elders who 'talk big' about their commitment to the Law but in practice do not follow its real requirements. It is the tax-gatherers and prostitutes who back away from any kind of commitment but later on think things over and comply with God's law. Jesus first obtains agreement as to who was the closer to God's will, and then returns to the example of John the Baptist. The tax-gatherers and prostitutes had heard his message and believed it. But not so the chief priests and elders.

Jesus is not really *praising* either category. He is merely pointing to the fact that the equivalent at that time of today's 'un-Churched' are frequently generous and given to practical charity, in a way that indicates a degree of living in accord with a faith which they will not even admit that they have. As for the other category, we have already stressed the importance of practising what you preach, of expressing your adherence to God's laws by word *and* example. Sanctimonious piety can be a sham and counterproductive. Jesus would have little time for the 'professionals' who merely render lip-service to his teaching.

The second parable, recorded by Matthew, was that of the wicked tenants of the vineyard. The vineyard is clearly the nation of Israel. The owner is God. The servants are evidently the prophets, and the tenants are the elders and religious leaders of Israel. They murder or beat up the owner's servants and then murder his son who has come to restore good order. The parable finishes with a note of prophecy: 'the stone which the builders rejected has become the cornerstone'. The point is taken by the chief priests who reach the conclusion that enough is enough. The teaching of this Jesus, whoever he is, represents a threat to their position.

Is there a link between the two parables? Are the vineyard owner's messengers whom he sends to collect his produce true prophets of his justice and truth? Are the tenants of the vineyard those who have power and influence in the business life of the nation, doing their father's will in their daily life, or are they those who simply show outward religion and talk? We might say that they would be happy to invite clergy to say grace at the banquet when the vintage is brought in from the vineyard, but resent any questioning of the way in which they carry on the business itself. In many aspects of industrial life today, the message of the gospel is considered quite irrelevant to the conduct of business, even where the high principles of etiquette and efficiency prevail. Responsibility towards share-holders can sometimes be used by management to offset any social obligation towards a well-deserving workforce. On the other hand industrial solidarity can blind union leaders to the effects of their action on the image of their firm, their industry or regional reputation.

Some business men say to us, 'You won't agree with this, bishop . . . ' and go on to describe their regular practice. Shop stewards have been known to ask, 'What does His Holiness know about that?' It often seems as though they acknowledge that Christian ethics are important in home and school, but have nothing to offer in the life of the market place. We are glad that sometimes they accept an obligation to give generously to charity; but it saddens us that introducing Christian values and concern for factors other than 'business reasons' are often held to distort good judgements. Thank God, other business leaders welcome visits from a bishop or an industrial chaplain or, more important, the presence of deeply committed Christians: they take seriously the ability of such people to hold up the mirror to those who make decisions in their business, to help them notice what they are doing to each other and to the community around them.

Being one of the owner's messengers risks rejection or being politely ignored as one of the external factors. There have been times when we have been invited to attempt reconciliation where there has been conflict or threatened closure of a factory. We have not been very successful in preventing such closures: but such Christian endeavour has sometimes helped to bring about resumed dialogue, increasing the prospects for improved industrial relations and job opportunities in the future.

Lord, give us courage and faith
to build up your Kingdom in the world of work.
Bless the efforts of peace-makers
and those working for reconciliation and justice
in industrial disputes.
Through Christ our Lord. Amen.

Saturday in Second Week of Lent
(Micah 7:14, 15, 18–20)

With shepherd's crook lead your people to pasture,
the flock that is your heritage,
living confined in a forest
with meadow land all round.
Let them graze in Bashan and Gilead
as in the days of old!
As in the days when you came out of Egypt,
grant us to see wonders! . . .
What god can compare with you
for pardoning guilt

and for overlooking crime?
He does not harbour anger for ever,
since he delights in showing faithful love.
Micah 7:14–15, 18

Micah was one of the twelve minor prophets; he came from South West Judah and lived in the eighth century BC. His book is a mixture of threats and promises, and from his prophecies he seems to have been a man of courage. He does not hesitate to proclaim the political disasters which will arise from the anger of Yahweh at the people's sinfulness and infidelity. Not merely does he denounce their practices of superstitious worship but he spells out in some detail their breakdown of morality.

Interestingly this breakdown is seen not just in terms of prostitution and the like, but in what today we would call social injustice. Yahweh 'thunders to the city' (Micah 6:9) against those giving short measure, those despoiling the land due to the people, those depriving the hungry of food. Then there is a great passage of faith in God who will forgive and save once again. The people must endure his anger for a while: they have deserved it. But with the prophet they may have faith in a degree of forgiveness which is without parallel. The Lord will chastise, not destroy his people, provided they return to traditional morality.

The prophet prays with pastoral imagery that the Lord will lead his people to safety once more, to a place of justice where their needs will be met. 'Living confined in a forest with meadow land all round' is a reminder that the Jews, after their return from exile, were isolated on land and in circumstances where it was difficult to provide for themselves. The prayer is for a return to the productivity of old, and to a level which evidently would astonish and surpass other nations. Micah says that God is concerned for the prosperity of the whole people and their need to walk humbly with their God.

There is much which can be written today about the importance of productivity. It must be related to market forces, we are told: which implies that it must at least be competitive with rival products, and as a rule must be related to needs. At times one must question the reality of the need, just how far need can be created by making a person aware and perhaps envious of another person's standards and possessions. But above all for success there must be resources and the capacity to produce, preferably in an attractive style.

It is not impossible to apply such concepts to spiritual values and growth, though it is always difficult to measure capacity for spiritual growth in the individual, just as it is in the community. There is a tendency nowadays to think in terms of different brands of spirituality. We hear of lay spirituality, clerical, priestly or religious spirituality, and of course of feminine and masculine spirituality. There is some basis in such distinctions, but not when an attempt is made to 'order' the different brands, as if they possessed their own hierarchy, as it were – with clerical spirituality at the top of the list.

Spirituality is a relationship with God, and the things of the spirit. The way that relationship is lived and developed will vary with differing circumstances: with age, being in secular surroundings in the 'world', or in the cloister. The difference does not depend upon environment, but there are undoubtedly varying circumstances and therefore ways in which we relate to God. Some would see it as differing degrees of difficulty. For example, a mother who is bringing up small children is unlikely to find the same time for meditation as she could when she was a student. In due time, when the children have left home, it will be possible for her to change gear again in her spiritual journey. In fact there are no circumstances in which God in his mercy and grace does not allow us to grow in our relationship with him.

Micah's God of unparalleled pardon never allows us to get beyond his reach, beyond the sound of recall. He knows the reality of our needs and is there to meet us, no matter how isolated we may feel, how disadvantaged in comparison with others. Britain is not the only land to have experienced a north/south divide in prosperity, health and opportunities. It is a reality here today and the divide may run through the same city, whether it be London or Glasgow. Such division has meant that different sections of our nation and of the world community have experienced very varied opportunities and in many respects differing standards of living. This can happen without people necessarily being thrown into enmity with one another. But recovery from such disadvantage, as Micah indicates, can be very difficult without divine assistance or, as we would say, unless there can be some help or investment by the 'have's' in the territory of the 'have-not's'.

In the recovery of spiritual health also, there can be need for help and encouragement from others, whose relationship with the Lord may, humanly speaking, have been less strained than is the case with those who feel that they have been marginalized. But the help that is offered must be related to the real areas of desolation which have been experienced, and not just consist of the lessons of spiritual life lived in very different circumstances and culture centuries ago.

The writings of the English mystics from the Middle Ages, for example, are small consolation, at least directly, to the poverty-stricken families in the shanty-towns of Latin America. The help we offer spiritually as well as materially must be related to the real needs of those less fortunate than ourselves, not merely the means of our clearing our consciences by passing on what we may decide is best for them, or most interesting to ourselves.

The key to sharing the riches God has given us, whether spiritual or material, without condescending to poorer people, lies in respect. A deep respect for those from other cultures leads us to listen to them with our whole attention and to expect to receive the riches which they have to give us. When we come in that attitude, ready for mutual giving and receiving, we begin to learn how to give with sensitivity.

Father God, pardon our guilt
and give us faithful hearts
that, without envy or selfishness,
we may work for the restoration of your Kingdom. Amen.

Group material

Starting points

- Which words from the Scripture Readings struck you most strongly this week?
- Recall the story from Monday's reflection, about the young priest who shared the suffering of the bereaved family.
- Does this remind you of anything in your own experience?
- When have you been able to share in someone's suffering?

Deeper reflection

1. 'I, Yahweh, search the heart, test the motives . . . ' Jeremiah 17:10 (Thursday).
   - How do you feel about the idea that God searches our hearts and knows our deepest secrets?
2. On both Tuesday and Thursday, we reflected on the readiness so often found today to judge people – whether the poor who cannot be blamed for their poverty or those who remain silent when accused, for good reason.
   - Have you ever found, in yourself, attitudes that judge people or go along with a negative impression?
   - How do such attitudes grow?
   - How can we counter them in ourselves? In our society?

3. We have also reflected this week on what it means to present the face of Christ to the world.
   - Where do you see the face of Christ presented today?
   - What are the qualities which should be reflected by Christians, both in personal matters and in social affairs?

4. If we look at people with the eyes of faith, we can see the face of Christ transfigured. We began this week with the gospel of the transfiguration.
   - Has there been anyone in your life recently in whom you have caught a glimpse of what it means to be transfigured?

Prayer

Look prayerfully together at an Icon of Christ.
- What do you see?
- Recall other faces of suffering in our world and share them with the group.

Pray for your heart to become more compassionate.

THIRD WEEK
OF LENT

*'Our experience has been that,
climbing out of our separate trenches,
praying together, increasingly sharing
in our Churches' lives together,
tackling together many of the great
human issues of Merseyside, has
brought us very close. It has indeed
been "better together".'*

Page 72

Opening the joint Church of the
Resurrection and St Bridget,
Cinnamon Brow, Warrington, 1989

Third Sunday of Lent

(Romans 5:1–2, 5–8)

So then, now that we have been justified by faith, we are at peace with God through our Lord Jesus Christ; it is through him, by faith, that we have been admitted into God's favour in which we are living, and look forward exultantly to God's glory . . . [This] hope will not let us down, because the love of God has been poured into our hearts by the Holy Spirit which has been given to us. When we were still helpless, at the appointed time, Christ died for the godless. You could hardly find anyone ready to die even for someone upright; though it is just possible that, for a really good person, someone might undertake to die. So it is proof of God's own love for us, that Christ died for us while we were still sinners.

Romans 5:1–2, 5–8

'Justified by faith': these words of St Paul were central to the Protestant Reformation which divided our Churches four hundred years ago. Since then much theological warfare has stayed in the trenches, still attracting hostile attention to statements and interpretations adopted centuries ago. These interpretations of the biblical words have themselves become entrenched. At least until quite recent inter-Church initiatives, they have fossilized attitudes, often preventing understanding of what is at stake for our brothers and sisters of the 'other' Church.

Our experience has been that, climbing out of our separate trenches, praying together, increasingly sharing in our Churches' lives together, tackling together many of the great human issues of Merseyside, has brought us very close. It has indeed been 'better together'. We know each other first and foremost as brothers in Christ. On occasions we have been through fire together; and this has bred a deep mutual trust.

So when we come back to the controversies of old between our Churches, we shall not expect to resolve all the differences swiftly, let alone by ourselves. What we do find is that we are much more able to understand and be sensitive to what is at stake for the other and of importance to him and those for whom he stands. We also have the consolation of finding that the central truths of our salvation, of the Trinity, of the Incarnation, death and resurrection of our Lord Jesus Christ, are our common possession. Our experience mirrors that of the second Anglican/Roman Catholic International Commission (ARCIC II), which has tackled the question of Justification and tried to get behind the old meanings attributed to the words in the Bible.

Today's verses from St Paul's letter to the Christians in Rome set forth one of the central truths which we share. Our salvation depends wholly on God's initiative. 'So it is proof of God's own love for us, that Christ died for us while we were still sinners' (Romans 5:8). He made the first move. The grace of God draws forth our faith and love. It brings us into a personal relationship. It is through our Lord Jesus Christ that 'we have been admitted into God's favour in which we are living' (Romans 5:2). This is sometimes translated as 'entering into the sphere of God's grace', where all relationships spring from his initiative. We are brought by his grace into what Jesus called the Kingdom of God, and which has helpfully been called elsewhere the kingdom of right relationships.

'The love of God has been poured into our hearts by the Holy Spirit which has been given to us.' So a kind of chain reaction is set up. God makes the first move towards us: not just once, but again and again. St John speaks of grace built upon grace: 'From his fullness we have, all of us, received – one gift replacing another' (John 1:16). As the Holy Spirit sheds abroad that love of God in our hearts, we in turn in our relationships, learn to make the first move.

In Alexander Solzhenitsyn's novel *Cancer Ward*, there is a character called Yefrem. All his life he has pushed the world around. Now his wife has left him. No friends come to see him. In the hospital ward he picks up a little blue book by Tolstoy, who says that love is the most powerful weapon in the world. Yefrem thinks to himself, 'There were some good ideas in that little book. Only they wouldn't work unless everyone agreed to start living by them at the same time.'

That is the objection which people have always raised to our Lord's way of love. Making the first move is not easy, especially for a person who does not feel responsible for any rift which may have arisen. The Holy Spirit can of course overcome that reluctance, whether it be between Churches or in personal relationships. But often we have our own human reluctance, not always conscious, to recognize or respond to the promptings of the Holy Spirit. There are times when we can help each other in this process of being open to the Holy Spirit.

A young woman, new in the faith, told her East London clergyman that she felt disheartened because she was not having the great spiritual experiences which some of her fellow Christians appeared to speak of. The clergyman reminded her of how she used to cut anyone dead whom she believed to have wronged her; and how she had told him recently that some days earlier she had gone downstairs to knock on the door of a neighbour's flat with whom she had had a row. 'You made the first move?' he asked. She agreed. 'And you say the Holy Spirit hasn't been giving you any great spiritual experiences?' he went on. 'What more profound change could you experience than that?'

Humility can lead to a proper hesitation. We are not to stroll casually into the presence of our Holy God. But the wonderful truth of the gospel is that through the death of Christ, sinners like us can be emboldened and come. Our prayer today is adapted from the words of the centurion in the Scriptures (Matthew 8:8):

'Lord, I am not worthy to have you under my roof;
just give the word and your servant will be cured.' Amen.

Monday in Third Week of Lent

(Luke 4:24–30)

Jesus came to Nazara and spoke to the people in the synagogue: 'In truth I tell you, no prophet is ever accepted in his own country. There were many widows in Israel, I can assure you, in Elijah's day, when heaven remained shut for three years and six months and a great famine raged throughout the land, but Elijah was not sent to any one of these: he was sent to a widow at Zarephath, a town in Sidonia. And in the prophet Elisha's time there were many suffering from virulent skin-diseases in Israel, but none of these was cured – only Naaman the Syrian.'

When they heard this everyone in the synagogue was enraged. They sprang to their feet and hustled him out of the town; and they took him up to the brow of the hill their town was built on, intending to throw him off the cliff, but he passed straight through the crowd and walked away.

Luke 4:24–30

As we read St Luke's account of this event, we feel the hardness of the attitudes adopted by others towards Jesus, and we sense the extreme danger he was in, if he were to persist. It is with sadness that he tells them that no prophet is ever accepted in his own country. Is it that they cannot believe that God could or would speak through someone whom they have watched growing up as an ordinary child? Or is it because he knows them too well and his well-informed challenge is too threatening, too near the mark for comfort? They hustle him and throw him out. He is back again in the wilderness, acutely conscious once more of the entrenched powers of evil.

What about ourselves and prophets in our own times? Are we willing today to recognize and accept prophets in their own country? Such a prophet might well be one of the 'wilderness' people we mentioned at the beginning of this book. He might perhaps be a disturbing colleague at work, a neighbour whose life-style challenges the assumption that religious people should expect to be reasonably prosperous; or perhaps a son or daughter who insists that God's way will not always support what seems to make our nation successful. We cannot in any case pretend that we easily listen to a prophet who comes from another Church or another group within society.

One of the great prophets of our time was undoubtedly Martin Luther King, the determined champion of racial justice and of non-violent means of resistance. He was shot because of the fears of those who felt threatened by him and by what he stood for. Yet there were many people who did accept his prophetic role. It was a remarkable feature of the Civil Rights movement in the United States that many white Christians from all our Churches gladly accepted the leadership of this black Baptist minister.

Another theme appears in what Jesus had to say in Nazara. Often God's cause had been maintained outside Israel. A widow from Sidon and a general from Syria had been touched by God's hand at a time when there were many widows and many lepers in need of help in Israel. This touched our Lord's hearers on the raw: they insisted that Yahweh, their God, could only be expected to work through Jews. They would not expect to receive anything of moral or religious significance from foreigners and from those of other faiths.

This loyalty to their own nation and its God-given destiny closed their minds to the possibility that God might work outside their ranks, and through unexpected, even unwelcome, people. They did not wish to be reminded that during a time of famine, the great prophet Elijah had depended for his life on the help of the Sidonian widow.

Our generation has seen very large numbers of Moslems, Hindus and Sikhs come to our cities, in addition to the Jews who have lived in this country much longer. Do we recognize that God has dealings with people of these other faiths? Are we ready to receive the help or insights which he may sometimes want to give us through them?

The story of General Naaman, related in today's Old Testament reading (2 Kings 5:1–15), has been a favourite in Sunday schools for generations. In a multi-cultural and multi-faith society, it poses a much more urgent question. Are we still to tell the story, with all the sharpness of its cutting edge? It seems that is what our Lord did at Nazara. Are we, in these fraught days, to call attention to war-torn Beirut, with the battle-lines drawn between Lebanese Christians, Syrian Moslems and Israeli Jews? Are we to assert, as Jesus appears to have done, that the story of Naaman gives us the lesson that God is at work through people behind each of those battle-lines? Do we take note that, when Naaman asked that Yahweh would forgive him if, whilst assisting his master the King of Syria, he bowed down in the temple of the god Rimmon, Elisha replied, 'Go in peace' (2 Kings 4:18–19)?

Relations with people of other faiths must begin with deep respect for all who are made in the image of God and worship the Creator God in their own way. Such respect means that we will join hands with them when common causes arise in the community, that we will enter into dialogue with them, and be ready to receive what in one form or another they may contribute to our lives. Dialogue means listening to one another with seriousness. It means being open to recognize an insight added to our understanding of an issue. It does not mean disguising one's own beliefs, or indeed that Christians should refrain from speaking with conviction about one's own faith.

True respect will include sharing the precious things of one's own faith, as well as being open to listen to the precious things of the other person. It calls us to act with generosity towards religious groups much less advantaged in Britain than the members of the Christian Church.

O God of Abraham, Father of Jesus,
you know the whole history of every human being:
help us, who know your Son Jesus Christ,
to grow in knowledge and obedience to him,
and to respect those of other faiths.
We discover you at work in many places we did not expect:
make us ready to give and to receive in the precious name
of Jesus Christ our Lord. Amen.

Tuesday in Third Week of Lent
(Matthew 18:21–35)

Peter went up to Jesus and said, 'Lord, how often must I forgive my brother if he wrongs me? As often as seven times?' Jesus answered, 'Not seven, I tell you, but seventy-seven times.'

Matthew 18:21–22

Back to forgiving again! You cannot open the gospels for very long without being faced with the need to be forgiven or the call to forgive. Here, Peter typically wants to pin down Jesus as to exactly what he means. He suggests what seems to him an almost absurd degree of repeated forgiving, generous in the extreme. Equally typically, Jesus is not interested in establishing a rule of thumb, as inevitably someone will produce the case requiring the forgiveness of a brother for an eighth time – or even one over the eight. He wants us to practise habitual forgiveness, the spirit of forgiveness: not seven times, but seventy-seven times.

If you read the full text, you will see that this episode is followed by the parable of the unforgiving debtor: the infamy of the one who has been forgiven so much, yet cannot find it in his heart to pass on some of that forgiveness to another person who is ever so slightly in his debt. For such an ungrateful mortal there would be no forgiveness until he had himself learned how to forgive.

We shall see in Holy Week how thankful Peter was for the emphasis on forgiveness. Recalling this parable of the man whose debt ran into millions, he would realize the scale of the forgiveness shown him for his denial of his Master who had loved him so much. In the light of that, he could not fail to forgive others for the so much smaller hurts inflicted on him. There is no comparable measure for the forgiveness of our Redeemer.

Some critics believe that all this forgiving simply makes people 'soft'. The truth is that love *is* very tough at times. It has to be. The unacceptable alternative is that we wash our hands of someone who has offended or hurt us. A good example of this was an inner city youth leader who had a great understanding of the trouble-makers in his club. He identified with them from his memories of his own boyhood in Glasgow. Whenever there was trouble in his club, he made it absolutely clear who was master: there was nothing soft about him. Quite often he would throw the whole club out: he made them all responsible for the activities of the 'awkward' squad and was not prepared to run a club merely for the youngsters prepared to say 'Yes sir' and 'No sir'. But when he had turned them out for nuisance-making, he would promptly follow them out into the street where he was prepared to have it out with them. They had previously met the kind of discipline which barred them from the premises permanently and rejected them utterly. Now they encountered a tough kind of love and concern, which would not give in to anti-social behaviour, but still wanted to know them and help them in the future. With forgiveness there is no permanently slammed door.

The critics sometimes go a stage further: 'Your religion makes things dead easy,' they say. 'You sin, you confess and you know that no matter what, you are going to be forgiven. So why worry how often? You commit the same sin over and over again, knowing that you can be forgiven whenever and as often as you want to.' That misunderstands the costly nature of forgiveness. Nothing moves us more earnestly to correct our faults than to see how much it costs someone who loves us to forgive such failings on our part.

This can be seen clearly in a marriage relationship. Talking to Christian couples, we do not find claims to superhuman standards. Rather, we hear frequent testimony to the fact that acceptance and forgiving enable partners to acknowledge to one another their failures and offences. There is more chance of building a lasting marriage when husband and wife recognize that they are human, than when they put one another on a pedestal.

When we speak of forgiveness in marriage, some people assume that we must be thinking of sexual infidelity. Indeed, that strikes at the root of marriage because it is a betrayal of intimate trust. Other less dramatic instances of breakdown may also lead a partner to believe that he or she has been deserted. When, for example, a husband assumes, as is often the case, that his job must take precedence over his relationship with his wife and children, he should not really by surprised if his wife ceases to believe him when he tells her that he loves her more than anything else in the world. A jet-setting business executive found it hard to believe that his wife felt unvalued and deserted, when, after only a few months of marriage, he took it for granted that they must move to another continent. He understood that promotion was at stake but failed to involve her in the decision. She felt so deeply about it, even some years later, that she could see no way of making a fresh start and instead set divorce proceedings in motion.

Our Christian talk of forgiveness may lead others to believe mistakenly that we attach little importance to these sins of omission or commission. We are not saying that at all. Read the whole parable in today's reading: the real point is that the master forgives an enormous and very serious debt, but that is the basis upon which he expects the servant also to forgive. 'Let us love, then, because he first loved us,' says St John (1 John 4:19). Christ's love for us took him to death on a cross.

In many marriages, realizing how great the cost of forgiving is sometimes stops the pretence that betrayals or desertions do not matter: it may lead positively to admitting to deep hurts and perhaps together to seek counselling help. In this way the forgiving calls forth a new energy in the one forgiven to work at healing what has been broken.

Look down, loving Lord, on your world,
divided and torn apart by sin.

We pray for the healing of broken relationships,
and especially for marriages which are in difficulties.
Give to each person who feels wounded
the courage to ask for help,
and the love to go on forgiving.
We ask it in your name, Lord Jesus,
who loved us first. Amen.

Wednesday in Third Week of Lent

(Deuteronomy 4:5–9)

Moses said to the people: 'Look: as Yahweh my God commanded me, I have
taught you laws and customs, for you to observe in the country of which you
are going to take possession. Keep them, put them into practice, and other
peoples will admire your wisdom and prudence. Once they know what all
these laws are, they will exclaim, "No other people is as wise and prudent as
this great nation!" And indeed, what great nation has its gods as near as
Yahweh our God is to us whenever we call to him? And what great nation
has laws and customs as upright as the entirety of this Law which I am
laying down for you today?

'But take care, as you value your lives! Do not forget the things which
you yourselves have seen, or let them slip from your heart as long as you
live; teach them, rather, to your children and to your children's children.'

Deuteronomy 4:5–9

The Book of Deuteronomy brings to completion the *Torah*, the Law
which gave the people of Israel their identity. Here was a vision of greatness
to put before their children and their grandchildren. The nation was not to
be famous for its military forces, nor for the strength of the pound or the
dollar, nor for artistic treasures or export figures. Their vision of greatness
was that others would say of their nation, 'No other people is as wise and
prudent as this great nation'.

We are inclined to regard laws and customs as a burden, restricting
freedom, hard to live up to. Jews saw, and see today, the *Torah* as the gift of
God's love. It offered signposts in the jungle of daily life, demonstrating
God's concern for every area of personal, family and community life. God

cared about the food they ate, the reliability of land-marks, even about the safety of the parapets of their houses. 'What great nation has its gods as near as Yahweh is to us?'

In certain important respects, following Christ is different from this way of Law. Often Jesus answered a question with another question, in order to make his followers think matters through responsibly and for themselves. Indeed, when people have been led to believe that Christianity is yet another code of law, with instant answers to all problems, they have often felt put off and have turned away. Some of the earliest Christians did, it is true, describe themselves as The Way: they were conscious of going on a journey. Christ had taken hold of them and was very close to them. He also provided signposts as an important help en route along the way. But the pilgrims had a strong sense that they also had to preserve their own keen sense of searching. Any invitation to come and join the journey included joining in the searching and questioning.

In a pluralist society, as Britain is today, the Church cannot and should not expect to lay down the law, at least not in the manner it used to in past centuries. But that does not mean that we should bow before those who claim that the Church should confine itself to 'spiritual' matters and stand back from other issues which effect the life of the nation, even if they are labelled 'economic' or 'political'. We are often told to concern ourselves more with the laws of morality but, as we have often seen, there can be a reluctance to include social justice in morality.

In all matters Christians have as much right as any citizen to join in the public debate; but we must be sensitive to the views of those from other faiths, whose background and traditions may differ from ours. It can at times be a very delicate balance between conscientiously held belief and respect for the beliefs of others. If in a particular case Christians hold that the common good would best be served by legislation, they have the right, and may have the duty, to work for this. But they must realize that in a pluralist society they have a duty to respect the honestly held convictions of others which differ from their own.

We cannot claim prior rights, nor pretend that we have an authoritative answer to every complex question, as if we had some heavenly hot-line. Such involvement by Christians in the market place or debating-chamber can be a bruising experience, but it is to be hoped that they will bring to these issues a concern for the whole person and the whole community, perhaps especially for those with the weakest voice.

Jewish parents have set a good example in teaching laws and customs to their children and grandchildren. We can learn much from them, especially in their respect for tradition. On the other hand some Christian parents seem afraid to pass on their faith and values to their children. Partly, this may be due to bad experiences of authoritarian teaching they may have received themselves. Partly, it may be due to confusion. Children themselves can be confused by the fact that parents tend to retreat at different speeds from old positions of discipline. Parental rights, of which we hear much, carry with them inalienable responsibilities.

We believe that we are on a journey with our living Lord. We have deep beliefs and values which we believe that we have learned from him. We have a vision of greatness for our country and of God's way: these we desire most earnestly to pass on. We know that it needs to be done with reason: in the end children, at least when they grow up, will choose for themselves. Best of all, we shall communicate what is precious to us by our example, by the way we treat each other in the family and beyond. We must not judge today by our recollections of yesterday; and we must be careful about seeking to impose upon tomorrow what merely seems best to us today.

O God of our fathers,
look with mercy, we pray you,
upon every home in our land.
Help us to make them places of loving communication.
We pray for all the children of today:
they have an ever-changing world to serve,
and questions to ask and answers which we never knew.
Give them, O Lord, a vision to inspire them
and a faith to sustain them.
We ask this, to your praise and glory. Amen.

Thursday in Third Week of Lent

(Jeremiah 7:23–28)

' *"My one command to them was this: Listen to my voice, then I will be your God and you shall be my people. In everything, follow the way that I mark out for you, and you shall prosper. But they did not listen, they did not pay attention; they followed their own devices, their own stubborn and wicked inclinations, and got worse rather than better. From the day your ancestors left Egypt until today, I have sent you all my servants the prophets, persistently sending them day after day. But they have not listened to me, have not paid attention; they have deliberately resisted, behaving worse than their ancestors. So you will tell them all this, but they will not listen to you; you will call them, but they will not answer you." Then you are to say to them, "This is the nation that will neither listen to the voice of Yahweh its God nor take correction. Sincerity is no more, it has vanished from their mouths." '*

Jeremiah 7:23–28

The word of Yahweh had come to Jeremiah, telling him to stand at the gate of the Temple and proclaim the Lord's message. He was to remind them of the covenant between God and his people and make plain once more their infidelity. God's prophets had been ignored and with the passage of the years the people's behaviour had grown worse.

Jeremiah himself had seen reforms, the reorganization of religious life, repairs to the crumbling Temple. He had thrown his influence eagerly behind the reforms of good King Josiah (2 Kings, chs 22 and 23), even though it had earned him the hatred of his own rural priestly family. The latter had seen the regulation, calling on every family to go up to the Temple in Jerusalem, three times each year, as a threat to their livelihood. It was also a challenge to the old ways they followed in the village of Anathoth from which Jeremiah came. In fact this requirement was to bring into effect a Book of the Law which was found when they were repairing the Temple. Some scholars have thought that this may have been part of the Book of Deuteronomy which we were reflecting on yesterday.

Today's Reading is part of the address Jeremiah gave, standing at the gate of the Temple. However great the crowds visiting the Temple, however great their enthusiasm for the building, Jeremiah himself was dismayed when he looked below surface appearances. What had happened to the vision that no other nation or tribe was as wise and prudent as the Jewish people? Our extract today finishes with the prophet's judgement, as he looks at the crowds about him: 'This is the nation that will neither listen to the voice of Yahweh its God . . . Sincerity is no more.'

Jeremiah was charging those who were enthusiasts for the Temple with treating one another unfairly, with exploiting the stranger, neglecting the widow and the orphan, shedding innocent blood, following false gods, stealing, murder, adultery, and perjury. It is a long list, but worst of all was that they compounded their offences by coming before God in the Temple and presuming to say, 'Now we are safe to go on doing all these loathsome things' (Jeremiah 7:10). Outward reforms and worship needed to be matched by sincerity in their daily lives. His challenge was addressed also to those whose youthful enthusiasms he had seen wither away as they had grown older. 'In everything,' he says 'follow the way I mark out for you' (Jeremiah 7:23): sentiments seemingly echoed in Harry Lauder's famous Scots song: 'Keep right on to the end of the road'. The prophet had learned the hard lesson of perseverance to the end, and was sharing it with the complacent frauds about him.

Are there dangers here for us today? In the Church? Beautiful liturgies, efficient reorganization, growth in church attendance and active membership, all these need to be matched by sincerity in the whole of our lives. Success is, of course, very difficult to assess before God. Not long ago a Minister of the Crown challenged the Churches to try to develop new theologies for a largely successful nation. Perseverance and consistency would take their place alongside sincerity in Jeremiah's response.

Perhaps we should begin ourselves by re-examining a keynote in our old theology, which has had a great deal to do with the achievement of economic success – the Puritan work ethic. At its root was a great Christian concept, that of *The Calling*. Today we speak of vocation, and centuries ago this was usually seen as a call to the religious life. However, the Puritans said that God called all people to use their God-given talents to change the course of events and to create wealth. Whether or not that produced a connection between religion and the rise of capitalism, as R. H. Tawney suggested in his book with that title, there is no doubt that it released powerful human drives and achievements in wealth-creation.

A generation of those who worked hard, with the glory of God in mind, gave way in time to others in which more and more people paid little or no attention to God's voice. The drive turned to personal achievement and to working for the benefit of a person's own family. Forgotten was the Caller who lay behind the Calling and his concern for the whole community, especially for those left out of the success and the wealth that was created.

The received wisdom of some very influential people in the City nowadays is to restrain the enthusiasm of those who enter the business world with the sharp questions which seemed so clear with Christ in the wilderness. We have heard of the leading banker, impressing upon an audience of fellow Christian business people how important it is that they should not allow Christian values to 'infect their decision-making about maximizing profits'. We believe nonetheless that there are many who would agree with Jeremiah about the importance of sincerity and morality in personal and business dealings. The doctrine of 'me first', or even 'us first', rapidly leads to a selective morality to protect the few, whom Jeremiah would surely have challenged.

Lord, whom we worship in the sanctuary,
help us to serve you faithfully
in our business and working life.
Give to us sincerity in all our actions;
and grant us, as we persevere to the end,
the integrity which we knew in our youth.
We ask this through him
who for the finishing of your work laid down his life,
even Jesus our Lord. Amen.

Friday in Third Week of Lent

(Hosea 14:2–10)

Israel, come back to Yahweh your God,
your guilt was the cause of your downfall.
Provide yourself with words
and come back to Yahweh.
Say to him, 'Take all guilt away
and give us what is good,
instead of bulls we will dedicate to you our lips.
Assyria cannot save us,
we will not ride horses any more,
or say, "Our God!" to our own handiwork,
for you are the one in whom orphans find compassion.'

I shall cure them of their disloyalty,
I shall love them with all my heart,
for my anger has turned away from them . . .
They will come back to live in my shade;
they will grow wheat again,
they will make the vine flourish,
their wine will be as famous as Lebanon's.

Hosea 14:2–5, 8

Hosea was a prophet in the northern Kingdom of Israel, after the split from the southern Kingdom of Judah, centred on Jerusalem. He started his public ministry about 750 BC. Those were dark days for a loyal follower of God, and Hosea had some sharp words for the way people turned to false gods, especially the worship of Baal, a collective name for the fertility gods of the old Canaanite religion. Yet in his prophecy as a whole, Hosea, like his God, emerges as a teacher of forgiveness, hope and love. But it was a difficult life in many ways for Hosea, whose wayward wife, Gomer, led a life of infidelity, symbolic of unfaithful Israel. We see more of this in tomorrow's Reading from the same prophet. Today our attention is focussed on the false gods and idols to which Hosea's hearers turned too readily when times were hard: a lesson not too difficult for us to apply to ourselves and the idols which attract us when times are, in another sense, too good, or at least not so hard.

Of course it is difficult for us, who have grown up in an age of immense scientific discovery, to understand what it must have felt like to be dependent upon the power of an idol. It can happen to most people almost unconsciously. We speak today of the danger of our being slaves to the mastery of advanced technology: some of that danger lies in the attractive wizardry of the object itself, whether it be for the saving of labour, for leisure, or ease of communication; much of the danger lies in envy at the possessions of others. For some years now we have seen the social implications of the 'chip', and much more besides. These can strike not just at employment but at the root of human relationships. We hear of new dangers threatening our world from what are called ecological crimes against the environment, and we grow concerned about the green-house effect and about damage to ozone layers, etc.

As we strive for ever-greater knowledge and power, we often seem to become more and more dependent upon energies and technological forces beyond our control. They make good servants but greedy idols, when we allow them to be our masters. Such is the speed of change, often irregular and unnerving, that the customary stable supports of our day-to-day physical existence can seem shaken and threatened. In just the same way our moral values are set at risk by the bio-ethical problems arising by the score from embryological research.

Are these perhaps some of the false gods of today, which are often through our human weakness changed from icons of mysterious beauty and wonder, pointing us to the living God, into idols mastering our desires and free will? Does the very shock of that help us to think ourselves into the situation of the hearers of Hosea? He spoke repeatedly of God's judgement of the people about their disloyalty. Yet at times it was they who felt abandoned, when one thing after another seemed to fail. This was as true for individuals as it was for the nation as a whole.

Suppose for a moment that you had moved into a smallholding, as a newcomer to the village. Suppose your olive trees and vines were failing to produce; suppose you longed to have a baby in a world where a woman was regarded as an utter failure if she and her husband were unable to produce a child. What more natural than that you would have turned for advice to a kindly old neighbour, who in all probability would draw on her life-long experience and say: 'I suppose that you have made your offerings to the Baal under the oak-tree? Oh, but you should. We have found nothing grows here unless the Baal is well pleased.' And if your child were sick, you can almost feel the shudder which would have gone through you, when you were warned of the power which the idol possessed.

Hosea points to the futility of the political alliance with Assyria and of putting your trust in the military; the imagery of riding horses refers to this. Yet in spite of all this our faithful God forgives. 'Yahweh's ways are straight, and the upright will walk in them' (Hosea 14:10). Although the individual at that time may have felt, like many an individual today, powerless in trying to understand, let alone play an influential part in something like foreign policy, yet the walking straight in the Lord's ways must mean that we try to exercise some responsibility, not just in our family circle, but in the society or neighbourhood in which we live.

The comfort of the false god of affluent self-sufficiency, or a hard-nosed concentration on company profits, without adequate regard for the contribution of the work-force, can amount to the worship of idols. Mammon can often be one of the Baals of today: but then so can envy.

Dear Lord,
God of human labour and advanced technology,
bless all people in their daily work.
You have given us the knowledge to produce plenty:
give us also the will to bring it within reach of all.
Through Jesus Christ our Lord. Amen.

Saturday in Third Week of Lent

(Hosea 5:15–6:6)

I shall go back to my place
until they confess their guilt and seek me,
seek me eagerly in their distress.

Come, let us return to Yahweh.

He has rent us and he will heal us;
he has struck us and he will bind up our wounds;
after two days he will revive us,
on the third day he will raise us up
and we shall live in his presence.
Let us know, let us strive to know Yahweh;
that he will come is as certain as the dawn.
He will come to us like a shower,
like the rain of springtime to the earth.

What am I to do with you, Ephraim?
What am I to do with you, Judah?
For your love is like morning mist,
like the dew that quickly disappears.
This is why I have hacked them to pieces by means of the prophets,
why I have killed them with words from my mouth,
why my sentence will blaze forth like the dawn –
for faithful love is what pleases me, not sacrifice;
knowledge of God, not burnt offerings.

Hosea 5:15–6:6

Today, in a further extract from Hosea, we are treated by the prophet to an exchange between his Lord and the people. Confident in Yahweh's loving forgiveness, they turn back to him, but more from fear than from true conversion of heart. Taking something for granted can lead to presumption without a profound or lasting purpose of amendment: 'like morning mist, like the dew that quickly disappers'. It is faithful love for which the Lord yearns, even though experience may lead to the conclusion that apparent repentance can prove temporary, and that freedom of will, subject to human weakness, can result, not in true liberty but in the taking of liberties – a very different matter.

That was the risk that the faithful and ever-forgiving Yahweh took with his people. It was the same situation with Hosea and his unfaithful wife, Gomer. Through this sad and bitter personal experience, the prophet came to appreciate the abiding love of God for his unfaithful people.

It was the first time that Yahweh's relationship with Israel had been described in terms of marriage. In the New Testament we find the beautiful reference fo Christ and his bride, the Church. Very different is the symbolism of the marriage of Hosea. 'Go, marry a whore' is the startling instruction given by Yahweh to the prophet, 'and get children with a whore; for the country itself has become nothing but a whore by abandoning Yahweh' (Hosea 1:2). Later, when she has been unfaithful to him, Hosea is once more told to reflect the love of Yahweh for his faithless people, Israel: 'Go again, love a woman who loves another man, an adulteress, and love her as Yahweh loves the Israelites although they turn to other gods' (Hosea 3:1).

Thereafter the story continues of Israel's infidelities, leading to today's passage, where the Lord makes plain that 'faithful love is what pleases me, not sacrifice'. Outward show of repentance is of no consequence without the sincerity of an undivided heart. We can imagine the cynical comments of Hosea's friends who saw him as an easily beguiled cuckold: 'He's too easy with her. She's making a fool of him. She'll never change.' Yet Hosea knew that in his imitation of his Master he had to go on, loving and forgiving and giving his unfaithful partner another chance. These are the beautiful words which Hosea passes on to the people:

'When Israel was a child I loved him,
and I called my son out of Egypt.
But the more I called, the further they went away from me;
they offered sacrifice to Baal
and burnt incense to idols.
I myself taught Ephraim to walk,
I myself took them by the arm,
but they did not know that I was the one caring for them,
that I was leading them with human ties,
with leading-strings of love,
that, with them, I was like someone lifting an infant to his cheek,
and that I bent down to feed him.'

Hosea 11:1–4

There must be many parents today who will find comfort in those words, recalling the love they have lavished on their children who seem, despite all the efforts and sacrifices made, unable to accept and follow the principles of religious faith they have sought to pass on. They will think of their grown-up children who have left home, gradually moved further and further away until it would seem contact is lost and there is nothing but memory. Yet, like the 'waiting father', in the parable of the Prodigal Son, their arms are outstretched in 'welcome home' and forgiveness if somehow the dearly-loved will remember and come back.

Alas, there are today many elderly persons, often living alone in flat-lets or rooms, left behind in inner cities when whole generations of their family have been moved away; and who think with love of their grown-up children who left them in search of work or adventure, and whose visits home have become increasingly infrequent. 'He's a good boy,' they tell their friends who enquire anxiously; 'he's got so much to see to these days,' they add in hopeful explanation. Such was the faithful and forgiving love of Hosea and of his Lord, who wanted love, not sacrifice, and knowledge of God, not burnt-offerings.

Knowledge of God, like love, has to grow. The convert or the penitent knows that there can be no boasting. It is the beginning of a journey which lasts a lifetime and beyond. We do not have to prove our faithfulness before we can set out. The journey begins with turning to face the undeserved love of God, knowing that the call is constant, as is the means to follow if the heart is willing. One young man, conscious that he was at the beginning of a new journey, prayed; 'Lord, I do not know where this will lead me, but I am willing to go with you. Please keep me willing.'

Jesus, lover of my soul,
forgive my unfaithfulness and shallow repentance.
Strengthen me as I go on life's journey in your company
towards the knowledge of God.
For your name's sake. Amen.

Group material

Starting points

- When have you ever found that working ecumenically means 'better together'?
- What examples of ecumenical partnership have moved or inspired you?

Deeper reflection

1. During this week we have explored some aspects of what repentance means, especially in our relationships with others. On Tuesday we talked of 'costly loving and forgiving'.
   - What are the times when you have experienced 'costly loving and forgiving'?
2. In your experience, does forgiveness call forth a new energy for healing?
   - How does it happen? Share an example.
3. What, for you, are examples of 'faithful love' such as Hosea talked of in the Reading for Friday?
4. The prophets called the people of Israel to repentance.
   - Who do you see as a prophet in our country today?
   - Are we all called to be prophetic?
   - What do we, in this society, need to be called to repent for?
   - How can we share in calling ourselves and others to repentance?

Prayer

Find a reading from the sacred writings of a non-Christian religion that speaks of God, and read it together.

- Pray for openness to learn about God from people of other faiths.
- Pray for those who are prophetic.
- Name them together and thank God for them.
- Pray today for the future of our society, and for the tolerance and compassion which we all need.

FOURTH WEEK
OF LENT

*'Never to be forgotten are those moving
occasions when someone who has been
very ill and in pain for a long time
confides, in response to an offer of
sympathy, that he or she would not have
had it otherwise. That weary but serene
smile is more than a hint of union with
the Saviour who in his lifetime on earth
showed himself as the suffering servant.'*

Page 100

Care of the Elderly, Kelton House

Fourth Sunday of Lent
(John 9:1–41)

As he went along, Jesus saw a man who had been blind from birth. His disciples asked him, 'Rabbi, who sinned, this man or his parents, that he should have been born blind?' 'Neither he nor his parents sinned,' Jesus answered, 'he was born blind so that the works of God might be revealed in him.

'As long as day lasts
we must carry out the work of the one who sent me;
the night will soon be here when no one can work.
As long as I am in the world
I am the light of the world.'

Having said this, he spat on the ground, made a paste with the spittle, put this over the eyes of the blind man, and said to him, 'Go and wash in the Pool of Siloam' (the name means 'one who has been sent'). So he went off and washed and came back able to see.

John 9:1–7

These few verses come at the beginning of an account of no less than 41 verses with which St John the Evangelist records in great detail not only the cure of the man born blind, but also the reaction of others to an event they could not explain but did not wish to believe. Set against the stalwart faith of the man who was cured, it is one of the most poignant episodes in the New Testament and should be read in its entirety.

First, we hear Jesus explaining that the man's blindness to that time was God's will, so that his power to cure may be revealed through what is to happen. Then the obvious change which has come about is questioned by those who remember the man's former condition. Not the same man, say the incredulous; but the man insists that he is. How did it happen? 'I did what he told me to do.' Then where is he, this miracle-worker? And the man, sensing trouble, replies, 'I don't know: I only did what he told me to do.' It all rings very true.

So he is taken before the Pharisees who raise the issue of someone doing things like this on the sabbath. That surely suggests that he is not from God. But the man sticks to his guns: 'He must be a prophet'. Clearly the man and his claim must be discredited. So they send for his parents who can only affirm the facts but offer no explanation. Pressure is applied on them, who back away from the real issue. 'Our son is old enough to speak for himself. Ask him.'

Once again he is brought before the Jewish officials who take him through the whole story once more. He praises God for his cure and is abused for his pains. How did it happen? What did you do to yourself that now you can see? 'I have told you already,' the man insists. 'Why are you so curious? Are you thinking of joining his followers?' This is too much and again they round on him. How can he make claims like this about someone who is clearly a sinner? 'Say what you like about him,' comes the reply, 'all I know is that I was blind and now I can see.' Nothing will shake his testimony: he is put out of the synagogue.

Then comes the loveliest touch of all. Jesus, hearing of this treatment, goes to find the man, and asks him, 'Do you believe in the Son of Man?' The answer is simple and straightforward. 'Tell me who it is you mean, and then I will believe in him.' 'He is speaking to you,' replies Jesus. The man says, 'Lord, I believe,' and worships him. 'I have come into this world that those without sight may see,' adds Jesus, but the Pharisees simply cannot believe that he is talking about them. 'Surely it is not *we* who are blind?' 'If you were truly blind, you would be innocent,' comes back the reply. 'Precisely because you are not blind but do not want to recognize the truth, you are guilty.'

Commentary upon such a full account is unnecessary. Lesson after lesson speaks for itself. Faith, unbelief and the task of establishing criteria for the miraculous or inexplicable are all things with which we have to live in the present age, where technology plays so big a part in the lives of so many. Just occasionally, even nowadays, we stumble on a case where the gift of faith is overwhelming.

When visiting a clinic one day, the priest who served as chaplain was told of the admission of a patient, renowned for a way of life which made him notorious in certain sections of the Sunday newspapers. It seemed that he was now incurably ill and had only a short time to live. The nurses were concerned for their patient, beset by the attentions of the popular Press. A few days later, when he arrived at the clinic, the priest was told that this dying man had asked to see him. When he looked into the room the man in bed, surrounded by flowers and messages, told the priest that he wished to become a member of the Church. Not surprisingly the priest was cautious. Was the man already baptised? 'No, please baptise me,' was the reply. 'It's not as simple as that,' explained the priest, scared of the man's passing emotions. 'I'll look in tomorrow and we'll have a talk.'

Next day the patient would brook no delay. 'But what about your beliefs?' asked the priest; 'I know you are very ill but belief is important for a Christian.' At the back of his mind was the thought of what the sensational Press would make of any apparent death-bed conversion, and the likely suggestion of pressure on the dying man. Then from the bed came a profession of faith: 'Don't ask me in detail. I believe what those nurses believe,' he said, pointing to a couple of Irish nurses by the door. 'All I know is that they're the best people I have ever met in my life. I want to finish up like that. I believe what they believe. Now baptise me.'

His wish was granted. A few days later, when the more sensational newspapers were recounting the man's more outrageous scandals of the past, the new Christian, a rosary round his neck, with his two nurses holding either hand, and serene in his final moments, went to God.

Lord God, Saviour and Redeemer,
grant vision to those who are dazzled by the 'bright lights'.
Give faith to those blinded by obstinacy.
In our search for truth,
be the light in our darkness.
Through Christ our Lord. Amen.

Monday in Fourth Week of Lent
(Isaiah 65:17–21)

For look, I am going to create new heavens and a new earth,
and the past will not be remembered
and will come no more to mind.
Rather be joyful, be glad for ever
at what I am creating,
for look, I am creating Jerusalem to be 'Joy'
and my people to be 'Gladness'.
I shall be joyful in Jerusalem
and I shall rejoice in my people.
No more will the sound of weeping be heard there,
nor the sound of a shriek;
never again will there be an infant there who lives only a few days,
nor an old man who does not run his full course;
for the youngest will die at a hundred,
and at a hundred the sinner will be accursed.
They will build houses and live in them,
they will plant vineyards and eat their fruit.

Isaiah 65:17–21

These words are from the third and last part of the book of Isaiah and represent both the Lord's prophetic words about his people and the response of the prophet. In an earlier chapter the Lord Yahweh reminds Isaiah of his covenant with his people: 'My spirit with which I endowed you, and my words that I have put in your mouth, will not leave your mouth, or the mouths of your children, or the mouths of your children's children . . . henceforth and for ever' (Isaiah 59:21). The prophet responds with that wonderful passage on the misson of the servant of the Lord: 'The spirit of Lord Yahweh is on me, for Yahweh has anointed me. He has sent me to bring the [good] news to the afflicted, to soothe the broken-hearted, to proclaim liberty to captives, release to those in prison' (Isaiah 61:1).

Much of the dialogue that follows is poetic and beautiful: 'My soul rejoices in my God, for he has clothed me in the garments of salvation, he was wrapped me in a cloak of saving justice' (Isaiah 61:10). But this is followed by a judgement of the nations, on 'the day of vengeance' when the time of retribution has come. In an astonishing exchange between the Lord and his prophet, the latter counters the charges of infidelity with fulsome praise of Yahweh's faithfulness to his people. He pleads for forgiveness for those who have turned away. 'Yahweh, you are our Father; we the clay and you our potter, all of us are the work of your hands. Do not let your anger go too far and do not remember guilt for ever' (Isaiah 64:7–8 [64:8–9]).

Then Yahweh replies, using the language of the vineyard which the prophet has previously employed: 'As when a bunch of grapes is found still to have juice in it, people say, "Do not destroy it, for it contains a blessing," so I shall act for my servants' sake. I shall not destroy them all' (Isaiah 65:8). At the day of judgement, those who have abandoned him, who have not listened when he has spoken, they will go hungry, and thirsty, and be put to shame. But not so his servants: to them he will give 'another name. Whoever blesses himself on earth will bless himself by the God of truth.'

So the Lord moves to the passage chosen for today. Once again it is important to see its setting. He is holding out a picture of messianic happiness which will not just be a patched-up world. The reward will be a new creation, supremely and eternally happy. The trials of the past will be no more: no 'shrieks' such as were foretold as coming from those condemned in the judgement of the earlier verses. New housing to live in; new vineyards to engross them. The joy of the faithful will embrace all that has been important on earth, 'matters of life and death', as we would say. Infant mortality will no more be a problem; and at the other end of the scale, no sense of anxiety nor dependence in a geriatric ward.

Improving statistics do not remove the sadness and anxiety constantly with mankind where life itself is uncertain. Nothing compares with the traumatic shock of sudden death, especially where children or young people are concerned. A profoundly moving example of this was the Hillsborough Disaster when so many Liverpool football supporters, most of them in the full bloom of young manhood, were suddenly crushed to death. The same shocked sadness can be true in such natural disasters as have been experienced in the last few years: air disasters, train crashes, the sinking of the cross-Channel ferry. Always there are salutary lessons to be learned, whether or not there are degrees of negligence. All these events and reactions to them underline precisely that uncertainty which the Lord promises to remove in the new creation.

The full course of life, usually thought of in terms of the biblical 'three score and ten', will be stretched to a century. This must represent eternal life, not just an increase in the number of geriatrics, kept alive by an improved standard of living, medical skill and scientific advances. 'And never again will there be an infant who lives only a few days.' In a shanty town which one of us visited recently, an improvement in the infant mortality rate was reported. Now just half of the children born survive beyond the age of five years.

It is not as if poverty lessens in any way the value which is attached to life. Life is valued as much among the poor and disadvantaged as among the rich and powerful, even though they may not be in a position to prevent the spread of disease or to counter the dangers of malnutrition. Today's Reading holds in front of us God's affirmation that life, in the setting of the new creation, will possess incomparable worth. Clearly Christians cannot support attitudes which contradict that.

Lord, grant us respect for human life,
for it is your gift which you entrust to us.
Give new hope to the depressed
and new purpose and direction to those who seek your Way.
Through Christ our Lord. Amen.

Tuesday in Fourth Week of Lent
(John 5:1–3, 5–16)

After this there was a Jewish festival, and Jesus went up to Jerusalem. Now in Jerusalem next to the Sheep Pool there is a pool called Bethesda in Hebrew,

*which has five porticos; and under these were crowds of sick people, blind,
lame, paralysed. One man there had an illness which had lasted thirty-eight
years, and when Jesus saw him lying there and knew he had been in that
condition for a long time, he said, 'Do you want to be well again?' 'Sir,'
replied the sick man, 'I have no one to put me into the pool when the water is
disturbed; and while I am still on the way, someone else gets down there
before me.' Jesus said, 'Get up, pick up your sleeping-mat and walk around.'
The man was cured at once, and he picked up his mat and started to walk
around.*

John 5:1–9

The cure of the sick man at the pool of Bethesda was yet another
example of a miraculous action by Jesus being challenged because it was
carried out on the Sabbath. The legalistic view was that the kind of help
required by the sick man to enable him to reach the waters was a breach of
the prohibition of work on the Sabbath Day. But the verses set before us
today are intended to focus our attention on the persevering patience of the
sick man, and the compassion and mercy of Jesus.

It was almost as if our Lord knew the man of old, perhaps from an
earlier encounter. He knew that the sick man, clearly weakened and disabled,
had endured his situation for a considerable period. 'He had been in that condition for a long time.' Presumably the man had come to terms with the fact
that without physical help there was no way he could get to the pool when,
for one reason or another, cures were taking place: presumably this refers to
special festivals, such as that for which Jesus had come up to Jerusalem. In
weakness or paralysis, he lay on a sleeping-mat and must have called out to
others for the help he needed and, in all probability, for alms as well.

In this translation (New Jerusalem Bible) at least, it seems clear that our
Lord's question was taken by the sick man as an offer of help to enable him
to reach the healing waters ahead of all the other invalids with whom he
found himself, herded together beneath one of the porticos. 'Do you want to
be well again?' may seem to be asking the obvious. One cannot help remem-
bering the remark of the leper to Jesus when he said, 'Lord, if you are willing,
you can cleanse me'; and our Lord replied, 'I am willing. Be cleansed'
(Matthew 8:2–3). Now, for the man lying on the sleeping-mat, always out-
paced by the paralytics who have helpers to call on, the response of Jesus is
just as instant: 'Get up and start walking.' But because it is the Sabbath, the
Jews who are present promptly rule the cured man and his healer 'off-side'.
'You are not allowed to carry a sleeping-mat around today. The law of
Yahweh forbids it.'

It seems that the cured man had no real idea who this great benefactor was. Jesus had quickly disappeared into the crowd around them and the man was innocent enough in identifying him to the mischief-makers who were cross-questioning him. We must not under-estimate his confusion and elation at suddenly finding his strength and full health restored to him. The contrast with the piteous condition in which he had lain so long must have been emotionally overwhelming. It was this and the man's enduring faith which had aroused the Lord's compassion.

Ill health and long term, perhaps life-long, disability can, as we must sadly admit, produce bitterness and complaint in a patient, but it is our experience that it can produce in many people a high degree of holiness. There are doctors who regard resignation in a patient as an unhelpful factor in a severe illness. Resignation may be coming to terms with reality. Just occasionally it achieves the grace of acceptance – being 'clad in the garments of salvation', drawn in some mysterious way into the mystery of Christ's sufferings on the cross. Never to be forgotten are those moving occasions when someone who has been very ill and in pain for a long time confides, in response to an offer of sympathy, that he or she would not have had it otherwise. That weary but serene smile is more than a hint of union with the Saviour who in his lifetime on earth showed himself as the suffering servant. In our own age, for all that has been achieved in pain relief, there are countless examples of uncomplaining and enduring faith.

Sharing in God's continuing creation, human skills have brought massively better health care to our generation. We would want to lift all this into what we mean by the ministry of healing. We thank God for improved methods of diagnosis, removing some of the mystery from nervous diseases and inexplicable physical complaints. There has been a tendency to play down the likelihood of miraculous divine intervention by cure or at least amelioration. Yet the Lord's power is no less today than it was at Bethesda nearly two thousand years ago. Neither is his merciful compassion.

Each year many thousands of pilgrims from this country make their way to Lourdes in the south of France. The annual pilgrimage from the Archdiocese of Liverpool is now two thousand strong. Included in that number are perhaps five hundred young people, who with medical staff and brancardiers (stretcher-bearers) care for the many sick pilgrims they take with them. The latter especially make this long journey more as an act of faith and devotion than in search of a personal immediate cure. These all will undoubtedly give a firm answer 'Yes' to the Lord's question, 'Do you want to be well again?' And it happens. Nearly always amongst the brancardiers and nurses are a few who came in the past as invalids. They know well to whom they wish to offer thanksgiving.

Lord, in your merciful compassion,
look with love upon those of your people
who for many years have endured sickness or disability.
Give them consolation in their closeness to your cross
and unfailing hope in your resurrection. Amen.

Wednesday in Fourth Week of Lent
(Isaiah 49:8–15)

Shout for joy, you heavens; earth, exult!
Mountains, break into joyful cries!
For Yahweh has consoled his people,
is taking pity on his afflicted ones.
Zion was saying, 'Yahweh has abandoned me,
the Lord has forgotten me.'
Can a woman forget her baby at the breast,
feel no pity for the child she has borne?
Even if these were to forget,
I shall not forget you.

Isaiah 49:13–15

Once again the prophet rejoices that the Lord's love for his people out-weighs whatever feelings of anger and vengeance may be aroused by Israel's infidelity. Even when at times it may seem that Yahweh has abandoned them, they should know in their hearts that he loves them because they are his own. This must be their consolation, no matter how sorely tried they may be. The immensity of God's love, infinite and eternal, and for each one of us individually, is – as people would say nowadays – 'mind-boggling'. It is beyond our comprehension. But it need not be beyond our faith.

Another quality of the Lord's love for us, existing to a unique, indeed infinite degree, is its unfailing character. It is always there, even when we may not be conscious of it. Such bleak and empty times as in today's Read-ing arise very often because we have become over-dependent upon the im-perfect human love of another. It is when this support fails, amidst injustice or neglect, that we are apt to question the Lord's unfailing love and compas-sion for us. History lessons in the past reminded us of that time when our forebears are alleged to have claimed that 'God and his angels slept'. Throughout salvation history there is record of the turning to false gods of affluence and power. This quickly becomes a denial of that very God who loves us with an everlasting love. That love allows us to choose freely, even if we misuse that freedom. His love does not stop. The prophets speak of a parent who sometimes punishes because he longs to welcome us back.

The exercise of this abiding and forgiving love is well described in this passage from Isaiah. Although people may place themselves in a position where they feel that they are forgotten, in fact the Lord continues to love them and care for them as a mother loves her own child. Nowadays we are often reminded of the feminine qualities in God, sometimes seeming to counter the all-male presentation of an infinite and eternal being whom we are accustomed to address as 'Father'. Indeed, it was in this manner that Jesus himself taught us to pray. The sensitivity on this issue may be due in great measure to an unhappy use of exclusive language, in liturgical worship and in preaching. Yet this short extract from Isaiah may lead us back to those of our English mystics who on occasion felt able to speak lovingly of God as mother.

'Can a woman forget her baby at the breast?' asks Yahweh: surely a rhetorical question in any culture. Few things arouse greater distress and criticism than child neglect by a mother. No closer bond exists than between a mother and her child. Husband and wife become two in one flesh, creating thereby a bond which cannot be broken. It is the same with motherhood. The Son of God himself took flesh from the virgin Mary. During the last War, a mother was informed of the death of her son in military action. When some well-meaning and sympathetic priest tried to help to console her by saying that he understood just how she must feel at that moment, she replied with a full heart that such feeling was beyond him. Nothing could compare with the bond between mother and child. She kept repeating over and over again: 'flesh of my flesh'. Nothing could compensate for her loss. It is not inappropriate to think in this way of the pain caused to the Lord when his children seek to break that bond with him, their loving Creator. Even then, the Lord will not let go. 'Look,' he says through the prophet Isaiah, 'I have engraved you on the palms of my hands' (Isaiah 49:16).

Over the centuries there have been countless examples of women who, at great personal cost and sorrow, have stood by their sons in times of suffering, misrepresentation, public disgrace and punishment. All too familiar is the voice of a mother, who on hearing of the death or disgrace of her son, who has earned in the world a reputation for crime or some worldly wickedness, has said in his defence, 'He was a good boy'. Some years ago now a well-known politician faked his own death and disappeared, but was later identified and arrested. His mother, a well-known local character who had been Mayor of her city, was deceived with the rest of us. Approached by the

Press, she rejoiced because he whom she had thought to be dead was alive. Then she added in his defence and without apology: 'He has always been a good son to me'.

The supreme example of this ever-present, never failing, love of a mother for her son is of course to be found in Mary, the mother of Jesus. Resolute in her grief, she remained at the foot of the cross until she was able to receive his dead body into her arms. This she did with the same love as she had suckled him as a baby at her breast. At the Last Supper, he made plain to us through his disciples that such unfailing love is asked of each of his followers. In his prayer for them to his Father he said: 'I have made your name known to them and will continue to make it known, so that the love with which you loved me may be in them, and so that I may be in them' (John 17:26).

Lord God,
we thank you for the maternal love
with which you have surrounded our lives.
Help us to be whole-hearted and faithful
in the love we show to others. Amen.

Thursday in Fourth Week of Lent
(John 5:31–47)

Jesus replied:
There is another witness who speaks on my behalf,
and I know that his testimony is true.
You sent messengers to John,
and he gave his testimony to the truth –
not that I depend on human testimony;
no, it is for your salvation that I mention it.
John was a lamp lit and shining
and for a time you were content to enjoy the light that he gave.
But my testimony is greater than John's:
the deeds my Father has given me to perform,
these same deeds of mine
testify that the Father has sent me.

John 5:32–36

The discourse set out at length by St John in writing of the reaction to Christ's cure of the sick man at Bethesda, deals mainly with the relationship between God the Father and the Son. In this way Christ's power to cure is explained. The passage from which today's verses are taken, stresses that he has been sent by the Father with the divine power to heal, and also that testimony to his mission has already been given by John the Baptist. Christ knew that some of his hearers had earlier sent messengers to John to check up on him; and John 'gave testimony to the truth' – not that he needed such testimony. His own words and the deeds he had performed spoke for themselves.

This attempt by the Jews to play off John the Baptist against Jesus was once again unsuccessful. Neither of them would speak of the other except in praise, though John in prison must have been puzzled by reports, and sought through his friends confirmation of the signs and cures reported to him. But always he speaks with humble reverence of the man, the strap of whose sandal he is unworthy to fasten. For his part, Jesus here testifies to the faithful witness John has given. 'He was a lamp lit and shining'; and for a time the people had been content enough with him. But then, as the truth of John's teaching brought them the hostility of their rulers and officials, their enthusiasm and commitment had waned.

The prophet Isaiah had foretold that John would prepare the way for the Messiah: 'Look, I am going to send my messenger in front of you to prepare your way before you. A voice of one that cries in the desert: Prepare a way for the Lord, make his paths straight' (Mark 1:2–3, quoting Malachi and Isaiah 40:3). 'John was a lamp,' says Jesus, a light which both attracts attention and shows the way. Yet the truth is that those who wish may turn their backs on the light, just as easily as they can shut out sound from their ears. That is as true today as it was two thousand years ago.

Naturally speaking, even a bright light can be obscured or become intermittent. The most sensitive and friendly of lighthouses cannot penetrate thick mist or fog. Nowadays most have an additional fitment which ensures that if visibility is reduced to a level where there is danger, a warning siren supplements the beam of light to acquaint approaching vessels of the presence of danger. John the Baptist's light was strongly audible as he cried out in the wilderness. Yet his words and the manner of his life called attention to his message far beyond the range of his prophetic voice. Today we need reminders and signs which point us to the light of the world.

In a church where the Blessed Sacrament is reserved, it is customary to have a sanctuary lamp where the lamp burns as a sign of the eucharistic presence of Christ. (There is a moving description of this practice in the final pages of Evelyn Waugh's novel, *Brideshead Revisited*.) The lamp, when lit, is a sign and is not far removed from the tabernacle where the sacrament is reserved. Some years ago a bishop, who observed this practice in the small private chapel in his house, placed the sanctuary lamp not in the chapel itself but on the wall of the corridor outside. When he was asked why, he used to reply: 'Every time I pass along the corridor, I need the light as a reminder that my Lord is really present within. In the chapel itself, he does not need the light to see if I am there.'

When we stumble and fall in life, it can be because we have disregarded the light, or because we have been blinded or distracted by other bright lights. Those who have to drive at night on wet roads will attest to the truth of that. It is also true with regard to the bright lights of life in the big city, which can lead astray those who have not learned how to keep their eyes on the road which is also the way, the life and the truth. Today we are reminded that John was the lamp. Jesus is our vision. His life, his teaching, his gospel is the way.

With the co-operation of the local authority, both our Cathedrals in Liverpool are illuminated when darkness falls. Very different in architectural style, they stand high above the city, as a sign of God's faithfulness and as a source of Christian service to those living and working in the community. But not as a static signal: rather as a sign of commitment to the spirit of the gospel. 'You are light for the world,' Jesus told the crowd who had gathered about him on the mountainside. 'No one lights a lamp to put it under a tub; they put it on the lamp-stand where it shines for everyone in the house. In the same way your light must shine in people's sight, so that, seeing your good works, they may give praise to your Father in heaven' (Matthew 5:14–16).

O Lord of light and salvation,
guide us safely in your way;
and help us to be true guides
of all who would follow us. Amen.

Friday in Fourth Week of Lent

(Wisdom 2:1, 12–22)

'For if the upright man is God's son, God will help him
and rescue him from the clutches of his enemies.
Let us test him with cruelty and with torture,
and thus explore this gentleness of his
and put his patience to the test.
Let us condemn him to a shameful death
since God will rescue him – or so he claims.'
Wisdom 2:18–20

Although the author of the Book of Wisdom is supposed to be Solomon, clearly the writer is a Jew, devoted to 'the God of our ancestors', and intent upon contrasting the ways of the godly and upright with those of his fellow Jews influenced by the views and culture of the pagan philosophers of Alexandria. So he starts by exhorting his readers to seek God and love uprightness, and thus sets out in some detail how the godless see life. It is from this quite extensive passage that today's verses are taken.

In some ways the taunt is almost the same as the words which rang in the ears of Jesus as he hung upon the cross: 'Let him save himself if he is the Christ of God, the Chosen One' (Luke 23:35). 'The chief priests and the scribes mocked him among themselves in the same way with the words, "He saved others, he cannot save himself. Let the Christ, the King of Israel, come down from the cross now, for us to see it and believe"' (Mark 15:31–32). Or the words can be seen almost as foretelling the form of the three temptations to which the devil subjected Jesus in the wilderness. This we considered earlier in Lent.

The succeeding verses add the notion of cruelty and torture, and the patient gentleness of the victim who has faith in the God who will rescue him. These words assume a prophetic force when applied to the supreme victim who suffered shameful death upon the cross. The patient gentleness of Christ was exposed to both cruelty and torture at the hands of the soldiers, who scourged him, mocked him and placed on his head a crown of thorns.

We cannot think about these verses without taking account of those tens of thousands who have endured torture and death rather than deny their faith in the Christ who pointed the way of suffering. A visit to the catacombs in Rome is a sharp, if romantic, reminder of the vast numbers of the early Christians who underwent the utmost cruelty and death. The apostles themselves were called on to give this same example. But we should not imagine that the so-called civilized culture of today, with its widespread religious indifference and political greed, has produced a reduction in the number of those suffering martyrdom and human degradation for the Christian faith. There are good grounds for claiming that the twentieth century has seen a larger number of people persecuted, imprisoned and killed for their religious beliefs than any comparable period of history.

Sadly the number of men and women, whose name and fate will never be generally known, will vastly exceed any list of those recorded in the official calendar of the saints or other rolls of honour. Each well-known victim of torture and cruel death serves as a reminder of those others who, as we say, 'are known to God alone'. In what sense dare we claim that 'God will rescue them'? Such confident faith in the power of the Redeemer against earthly odds makes sense only in terms of eternal values.

When Pope John Paul came to this country to visit Archbishop Robert Runcie at Canterbury, we were both present for that historic service in the Cathedral. Afterwards, before making a visit together to the place where St Thomas Becket was martyred, they paid a visit to the Chapel of the Martyrs of the Twentieth Century. There candles were lit in honour of twelve well-known Christians whose death was symbolic of the suffering of many others who lost their lives in the same struggle for truth and religious freedom. Thus were linked together the memory of Archbishop Luwum, Anglican Primate of Uganda, Archbishop Oscar Romero, Archbishop of San Salvador, Dietrich Bonhoeffer, Martin Luther King, and others who somehow stood for many in their brave defence of their faith at the cost of their lives. It was a most significant moment in the history of ecumenical understanding.

The butchery of the past has not disappeared. It has been supplemented by cruel scientific and psychological forms of torture to break the spirit of a victim; to brainwash or extract false confessions which incriminate others as well as being customarily a prelude to execution. These terrible techniques deprive the prisoner of self-respect and even of the conscious decision to offer defiance in confronting attacks upon the Church. There are already many wonderful accounts of courage in face of this kind of cruelty. The barbarity of the Inquisition is in many instances surpassed by the tortures of today.

A group of young worker prisoners in Latin America, arrested and herded together in a cell, awaited the inevitable questioning and torture. Eventually a young woman was taken out by guards and called out to the others to pray for her that she might retain silence. For over an hour the others heard her cries of agony from the cell to which she had been taken. When finally, shattered, bleeding and humiliated, she was flung back into the common cell with the others, she managed to say, 'I told them nothing' before dying from her ordeal.

Another tragic example was that of the young Hungarian priest, Andrew Zakar, serving as Private Secretary to Cardinal Josef Mindszenty, the Primate of Hungary in the post-war years. Andrew, who anticipated his own likely eventual arrest, endeavoured by prayer and physical penance to prepare for the ordeal ahead. When he was arrested in mid-November 1948, he lasted just four weeks before they broke him and extracted a false confession from him to incriminate his Cardinal. At a public trial in February 1949, they sat together, empty husks of their former selves, to receive long terms of imprisonment. The Cardinal was eventually freed. Andrew Zakar was kept 'in detention' until his death a few years ago, never having regained his mental balance. Did·he hear those verses from the Book of Wisdom, which we read today, during that month of endurance before they broke him?

> Lord, we pray for all those who suffer
> for the Christian faith we share with them.
> We pray for all prisoners of conscience
> whose 'gentle patience is put to the test'.
> Grant them strength and freedom,
> and an eternal reward for their steadfastness.
> Through Christ our Lord. Amen.

Saturday in Fourth Week of Lent
(Jeremiah 11:18–20)

Yahweh informed me and I knew it; you then revealed their scheming to me. I for my part was like a trustful lamb being led to the slaughterhouse, not knowing the schemes they were plotting against me, 'Let us destroy the tree in its strength, let us cut him off from the land of the living, so that his name may no longer be remembered!'

Jeremiah 11:18–19

For his faithful reminders to the House of Judah and the House of Israel, the prophet Jeremiah soon incurred the criticism and often the active dislike of those about him. There were those who almost resented his presence because they saw in his fidelity and goodness a reproach to their own way of life; and there were those who felt bitterly about him because he usually proved to be right and they were unable to discount his warnings. His demands for reform would inevitably mean a change in their lives. So if that was uncomfortable, at first it was enough to disbelieve what he said. When that proved them wrong, they plotted to silence him.

On this occasion God revealed their plotting to Jeremiah and he felt shattered. Even those he thought his friends and allies were lined up against him, so that he scarcely knew where to turn for comfort and security. He thinks of himself as 'a trustful lamb', being led off to the slaughter-house. Despite all the so-called humane methods of killing animals even today, it is hard to remain totally unmoved at the sight of animals being led 'all trustingly' to the abattoir. Even more terrible are those photographs from the last War of Jewish men, women and children, being loaded into cattle-trucks bound for the labour-camps, where the next steps were into death chambers and incinerators.

In these plaintive words of Jeremiah, Christians have recognized a prophecy of Christ himself. As a 'trustful lamb', Jeremiah is a fore-runner of the 'lamb of God' who was to take away the sins of the world. He was to be led to the 'slaughter-house' of Mount Calvary. Perhaps the difference between the Lord and those being led to their death is that, although they must have been reasonably sure of the fate which awaited them, Jesus Christ, the Son of God made man, knew full well of the agony he must undergo to achieve his Father's will. What he knew as the Son of God did not lessen the terror he must have endured, in advance as well as at the time, in his fully human agony.

Undoubtedly the lamb was spoken of in the Old Testament as a sacrificial victim. In the New Testament, where pastoral language abounds, the lamb is shown also as the vulnerable animal dependent upon the saving care of the shepherd. On the shore of the Sea of Tiberias, the risen Christ charges Simon Peter to 'feed my lambs', so that in those final verses of St John's gospel we find the word being applied to the believers of Jesus, to Christians. In this sense, to be a trustful lamb implies a confidence and belief which may involve some measure of sacrifice. It is not a blind trust, but is based on the love and power of the shepherd, who protects but does not retaliate when under attack.

In life today we often speak of seeing a thing 'coming' quite a long way in advance. This may be due to experience or we may have been able to foresee an almost inevitable consequence. It is when no avoiding action is possible, to stave off some misfortune or hardship, that faith is often put to the test.

In industrial circumstances it is often said that a factory is doomed from the time when the directors or management of a business decide not to utilize profits to reinvest in the works with renewed machinery, new technology, etc. The knowledgeable workforce knows it is only a matter of time before the forthcoming closure is announced. In the intervening period the workforce can be cast almost in a sacrificial role, since there is little they can do to improve productivity without technology. Their days are numbered and they face the eventual charge of low productivity, and the transfer of their work and livelihood to another factory elsewhere, where investment has been made in new equipment for a new workforce. In such circumstances the preservation of industrial harmony based on trust is, at best, very difficult.

A more personal example is where a patient is diagnosed as having an incurable, probably terminal, disease; but the news is given only to the wife or husband or the next of kin. Such secrecy can effect a mockery of the mutual trust which the sick person has hitherto always known with his or her family and friends. We have dealt with the issue of bereavement elsewhere. But increasingly it is becoming clear that a suppression of honesty, total or just 'economy of truth', often deprives dying persons of the openness and love they knew. For instance, one of us was visiting a vicar who was only a few weeks away from death. He and his wife had not talked about it at all; with his wife's permission, it was put to him, 'You must be anxious'. The bottled up feelings came tumbling out: he knew perfectly well that he was dying. His great anxieties were about how his wife would manage. They started to talk trustfully. They were able to make joint plans for her future and to face his death very openly and together.

Such sharing of truth can be an immense help in preparation for the supreme meeting with Christ, the 'trustful lamb', who went forward to death to rid us of many of our fears and to open the way for us to eternal life.

Lord God, our Father,
open our eyes to what you wish to reveal to us.
Give us understanding of the sacrifice you ask of us,
and the courage and faith to accept your will;
for the love of your Son, Jesus Christ our Lord. Amen.

Group material

Starting points

- Recall Monday's reading from Isaiah.
- What do you like about Isaiah's vision of 'a new heaven and a new earth'?
- What would you like to add to it?

Deeper reflection

1. This week, the Readings and reflections have explored aspects of love. On Wednesday, Isaiah used the image of a mother's love to describe how unfailingly God loves us.
   - What, for you, is at the heart of a mother's love?
   - Do you find the idea of the maternal love of God for us helpful?
2. This week also contained two stories of healing. Jesus restores the sight of the man born blind and heals the man at the pool of Bethesda.
   - What struck you about these stories?
   - Why did Jesus heal these men?
   - Do we take seriously enough the healing power of Jesus?
3. On Friday, we saw how love sometimes requires the ultimate sacrifice of life itself.
   - How do you feel about the courage shown by martyrs?
   - Which of those who have given their lives for their faith have moved or inspired you?

Prayer

Around a lighted candle, recall some of the places in our world where people suffer for their faith.

Recall some of the people in whom the light of faith has shone brightly in our world . . . martyrs or people who are still living . . . and thank God for them.

Pray for the courage to be, like John the Baptist, 'a lamp lit and shining'.

Say together the prayer from Thursday.

FIFTH WEEK
OF LENT

'We quickly saw for ourselves in South
Africa the importance of our Lord's
words, "The truth shall set you free".
We were greatly encouraged by much
that we saw of church life, standing and
suffering with people in their struggle
for freedom. We were impressed by the
ability and maturity of so many of the
Churches' black leaders, and by the
vigour and joy of their worship.'

Page 124

With Archbishop Desmond Tutu,
in Cape Town, May 1989

Fifth Sunday of Lent

(Romans 8:8–11)

Those who live by their natural inclinations can never be pleasing to God.
You, however, live not by your natural inclinations, but by the spirit, since
the Spirit of God has made a home in you. Indeed, anyone who does not
have the Spirit of Christ does not belong to him. But when Christ is in you,
the body is dead because of sin but the spirit is alive because you have been
justified; and if the Spirit of him who raised Jesus from the dead has made his
home in you, then he who raised Christ Jesus from the dead will give life to
your own mortal bodies through his Spirit living in you.

Romans 8:8–11

It seems generally agreed that Paul wrote his letter to the Christians in
Rome when he was in Corinth in the year 58. He was to some extent preparing them for his coming, as at that time he was planning a missionary journey to Spain via Rome. In fact when he went on to Jerusalem he was
arrested, and it was AD 61 before at last, after shipwreck, he was delivered
to some form of 'house arrest' in Rome. The letter to the Romans was a fairly
full treatment of his main theme, the salvation of the Gentiles through faith
in Jesus Christ. In this passage Paul is stressing the distinction between the
natural life of man, descended from Adam, and man vitalized by the indwell-
ing of the Holy Spirit.

In his writings St Paul had much to say about the 'flesh' and the 'spirit'.
It is important for us to try to appreciate his distinction between man's lower
nature, with its 'natural inclinations', and the new nature which the Spirit of
Christ brings. Otherwise we can be misled into thinking that Paul is separat-
ing the 'spiritual life' from the whole round of earthly life which the Christian is called upon to lead. At the end of today's Reading he stresses that
God 'will give life to your own mortal bodies through his Spirit living in
you'. That speaks of making our body, mind and spirit what God created us
to be: in a modern phrase, 'to be more fully human'.

In this chapter of Paul's letter, the Spirit inspires us to pray *'Abba,*
Father', the same intimate word as was used by Jesus. He energizes us
beyond our own strength to live by God's commandment. The Spirit within
us looks forward with hope to life and peace, when others see division and
death. He gives life to our own mortal bodies, enabling our senses to be
more aware of God's whole creation, and sensitive to others around us. Paul
describes the Spirit as living in us, making his home in us, not simply coming
as an occasional visitor when we have a spiritual 'high'.

All this is rather similar to the ideas in the famous phrase in St John's gospel about being 'born again', born of the Spirit. In more recent years that phrase 'born again' has been hi-jacked to enable Christians who have experienced one particular route to faith, and one understanding of how we are to live, to claim that they are 'born-again Christians'. Not unnaturally other Christians react against this description and may thereby miss out on an important understanding of the Holy Spirit. They are afraid of being 'got at' by these enthusiasts and of being forced into religious fanaticism. For them the mere mention of the Holy Spirit is enough to invite them to raise their guard.

In his autobiography, *Surprised by Joy*, C. S. Lewis described the feeling of keeping his guard up and the moment when he decided to let it down:

I was going up Headington Hill in Oxford on the top of a bus. I became aware that I was holding something at bay, or shutting something out. Or, if you like, that I was wearing some stiff clothing, like corsets, or even a suit of armour, as if I were a lobster. I felt myself being there and then given a free choice. I could open the door or keep it shut; I could unbuckle the armour or keep it on. Neither choice was presented as a duty; no threat or promise was attached to either, though I knew that to open the door or to take off the corset meant the incalculable. The choice appeared to be momentous, but it was also strangely unemotional. I was moved by no desires or fears. In a sense I was not moved by anything. I chose to open, to unbuckle, to loosen the rein.'

If we are to have for ourselves the enlivening experience described by St Paul, we need to unbuckle the armour around us, as C. S. Lewis did. This can need to happen more than once, for there is, especially amongst males, a protective habit of keeping strict control of our feelings. The ancient Greeks spoke of *accidie*: that has been translated as sleeping sickness, or indolence of heart, preferring to live in a half-life, searching occasionally for a stimulant. *Accidie* is not the same as laziness. Indeed, there are those who keep themselves busy, working all hours, in order to keep their imagination under control, losing themselves, as we say, in work.

Ronald Knox speaks of *accidie* as tepidity, when somehow the shine in one's way of life is no longer there and the exercise of one's calling becomes routine. That is when we need the sparkle of the Holy Spirit. Unbuckling to admit the Spirit means letting go of the control with which our imagination or initiative is restricted. It means opening our imagination and awareness to let him kindle our senses so that we may feel more sharply what is going on inside and all around us. It means that the Holy Spirit is free to move between us and other members of the Body of Christ, so that we may start to listen to the insights they can bring to us.

We are often afraid to unbuckle our armour of self-protection to let in the Holy Spirit, lest instead we merely allow irrational forces to impose strange ideas on us from outside. Yet the promise is that 'he who raised Christ Jesus from the dead will give life to your own mortal bodies through his Spirit living in you'. That beckons us to new adventure, enables us to develop our potential. God does indeed want us to be fully human. At the end of each day we could try to reflect on which events have that day brought us more alive, and which have deadened us, making us reach for that discarded armour.

Holy Spirit,
we thank you for the variety you inspire
in your creation,
in our sisters and brothers,
in our mortal bodies.
Fearfully but trustingly we open our defences
to see with your fresh awareness,
to act with your new energy,
and to share with you in your continuing creation.
We make this prayer through our Lord Jesus Christ,
the first-born of all creation. Amen.

Monday in Fifth Week of Lent
(John 8:1–11)

The scribes and the Pharisees brought a woman along who had been caught committing adultery; and making her stand there in the middle they said to Jesus, 'Master, this woman was caught in the very act of committing adultery, and in the Law Moses has ordered us to stone women of this kind. What have you got to say?' They asked him this as a test, looking for an accusation to use against him. But Jesus bent down and started writing on the ground with his finger. As they persisted with their question, he straightened up and said, 'Let the one among you who is guiltless be the first to throw a stone at her.' Then he bent down and continued writing on the ground. When they heard this they went away one by one, beginning with the eldest, until the last one had gone and Jesus was left alone with the woman, who remained in the middle. Jesus again straightened up and said,

'Woman, where are they? Has no one condemned you?' 'No one, sir,' she replied. 'Neither do I condemn you,' said Jesus. 'Go away, and from this moment sin no more.'

John 8:3–11

Today's Reading presents a vivid and dramatic scene. We suggest that you take a little longer with your reflection today, and try to put yourself in the picture. In this way you may gain the full lesson which the evangelist is putting before you. First, suppose you are the woman; then do the same, supposing you are Jesus. Let your imagination take you into that Temple court. When you have thought yourself into the principal characters, for a further exercise you might imagine yourself amongst the Pharisees and scribes who accuse her, in the hope of also involving Jesus in opposition to the Law.

Suppose you are the woman . . . She was terrified, as well as ashamed, by the time they had dragged her in front of Jesus: she had been roughly man-handled. 'Caught in the act,' says one, 'she cannot be allowed to get away with it. She's just the type of woman who sets out to break up other people's marriages.' 'We shall make her an example,' says another self-righteously, 'especially just now when we should all be standing together to stop this landslide of immorality'. The faces around her now are hard, some excited not only to have caught her but to test this Jesus out on the Law of Moses. Almost certainly the man who had been eager enough for their affair had disappeared by this time. Now she must face retribution on her own. The secrecy of the act had been exposed. Her shame is paraded before the crowd which has gathered. Her feeling of being abandoned and defenceless, all on her own, is made acute by the fact that no one is even treating her as a per-son . . . until she is brought before Jesus. He begins to write with his finger on the ground, perhaps in embarrassment, perhaps sensing the trap, search-ing for time.

Then he looks round at the excited group gathered about him, and says quietly, though with steel in his voice: 'If there is one among you who is guiltless, who has not sinned . . .' None can face that challenge: gradually the crowd melts away and she is left alone with him. Her trembling ceases. She is calmer and able to begin thinking again. The immediate danger seems to be over. Now there is greater warmth and obvious understanding in his voice. She senses what she has previously been denied; that she is being treated as a person. He is not condoning what she has done but there is understanding and mercy in his words. And she herself understands more clearly the seriousness of what she has done, and the betrayal of love which adultery is. As he says to her, 'Go away now and sin no more,' she has no doubt in her mind about how she wishes to live in the future.

Suppose you are Jesus . . . That circle of hard, self-righteous faces was an unlovely sight. Adultery is unlovely too; a wrecker of homes and of trusting relationships. But this punitive witch-hunt, refusing to see her in any sense as a human person, with human weaknesses and in conditions which may have helped to force her into this way of life, this is very ugly too. He tries to see behind the hostile faces, for so often fear fuels the anger of such a moment. Some seem trapped by their loyalty to the Law and by an honest wish to protect the marriage bed. At the same time there are others willing to condemn the woman for what they would regard in a man as youthful indiscretion.

Jesus realizes quickly that he is being deliberately put on the spot. What is his attitude to the sacred Law? Writing on the ground with his finger gains him a certain amount of time, almost as a cooling-off period. When at last the others have gone, he sees that she is not a man-eating seductress but a weak woman who has been carried away by desire. How can he best support these new stirrings within her to do what is right in the future? He knows the power forgiveness can have and that somehow she has the ability to respond when he says, 'Go away and don't sin any more'. He realizes that since he has declined to condemn her, now he will be even more the target for their hatred and abusive criticism. In all the grape-vine repetition of his words and attitude, the fact that he has told her not to sin again is more than likely to be omitted.

In our day too we fear what seems a landslide of sexual immorality. There is a natural longing that the Church by its words and actions will bring it to a halt. When we think about how we can help to achieve that, we need to be clear that the basis of Christian morality is love, not fear. Our young people are growing up in what has become known as 'The Pill paradise'. On the other hand, the fear of AIDS has given a jolt to promiscuous behaviour and led to a change in some people's moral life-style. But a morality based on fear keeps desires buried and unacknowledged. Not behaving in particular ways, because someone else tells you that something terrible will happen to you, fails to touch the deep springs where you decide what is really asked of you and what you really want. That is where morality begins.

Love is the basis of human morality. It treats other people with respect. When a deep trust develops in a partnership, a lasting and faithful relationship is called for. 'Marriage for keeps' is a cause worth fighting for. It provides a trusting environment in which the healing of wounds and of strained relationships becomes possible. Marriage needs signposts and warning fences to protect that trusting environment. Our hope and prayer is that better education and marriage preparation, begun from the earliest days in the home, will encourage young people to keep themselves for one partner. Yet when people do become caught up in desires which threaten relationships within marriage, we pray that the Church will reflect the same merciful, understanding and forgiving attitude which Jesus adopted towards the woman taken in the act of adultery.

O Lord, our faithful redeemer and friend,
help us to stand firmly for fidelity in marriage;
may our homes be places of acceptance and trust.
Help us also to know how to stand
for the mending of broken lives
and the restoration of love.
We ask this of you, who know the perfect love of the Trinity
with the Father and the Holy Spirit. Amen.

Tuesday in Fifth Week of Lent
(John 8:21–30)

So they said to him, 'Who are you?' Jesus answered:

'What I have told you from the outset.
About you I have much to say
and much to judge;
but the one who sent me is true,
and what I declare to the world
I have learnt from him.'

They did not recognise that he was talking to them about the Father. So Jesus said:

'When you have lifted up the Son of man,
then you will know that I am He
and that I do nothing of my own accord.
What I say
is what the Father has taught me;
he who sent me is with me,
and has not left me to myself,
for I always do what pleases him.'

John 8:25–29

The discourses in St John's gospel lift a corner of the curtain to reveal what was the driving force for Jesus in his life on earth. Repeatedly he speaks of the 'one who sent me'. The secret of what fills him with renewed hope, in face of many disappointments, lies in those many moments when he takes time to be alone with his Father. With him Jesus talks over their divine and costly plan for the healing and redemption of the world.

In today's Reading Jesus finds himself in the thick of controversy. His values are different from those of the world to which he has been sent. He realizes that the Jews, to whom he is speaking, will lift him up in crucifixion, but despite the human fear and revulsion he must have felt, he will not be deflected. It is a course which is pleasing to his Father and that is motivation enough. It is this which sustains him under the constant pressure of his mission. At times he does not seem to have time enough to eat. Again he discloses his inner motivation. When his disciples press him to have something to eat, his reply is, 'I have food to eat that you do not know about . . . My food is to do the will of the one who sent me, and to complete his work' (John 4:32, 34). Jesus is marching to a drumbeat which no one else can hear: it is the voice of the one who sent him.

After Easter he confers this same sense of mission on his disciples: 'As the Father sent me, so am I sending you' (John 20:21). This does not lift us out of this world, but it means that in our response to this mission which he gives us, we too are going to need the motivation which inspired him and a set of values which may well differ from those guiding the lives of the people to whom we are being sent.

The first vocation or calling to each of us Christians is to make good our baptism, entering into Christ's death and resurrection. Each of us can be aware of his presence with us as we go on life's journey, responding to our particular calling. There has in recent years been a very healthy emphasis on the calling of the whole people of God to various ministries. Through our baptism we are called to holiness and to share in the mission which Christ left to his followers. This is what is called the mission or priesthood of Christ's faithful people.

The manner in which this role is carried out, especially if done in the name of the Church, may well be regarded as ministry. It is distinct from the ordained ministry to which some few of the faithful are called, though clergy and laity may well collaborate in the mission of the Church. Lay people are in the front line in the world of daily work. Even though the task or role may be in 'un-churchy' things, it can well be ministry and be pursuit of holiness. The varied talents of the laity are all needed if the local Christian community is to be the varied and effective body God wants it to be.

It would be a mistake to imagine that because there is this more fully developed understanding of lay calling or ministry, there is less need or value to be attached to holy orders – episcopate, priesthood and diaconate. And the same is true with regard to a vocation to the religious life, male or female. All are needed, and there is of course a relationship between the different forms of ministry, ordained or lay. In his letter *Christifideles Laici*, Pope John Paul II has written recently that the ordained ministry expresses and brings about 'a sharing in Christ's priesthood that is essentially different from the laity's sharing. Yet the ministerial priesthood is fundamentally directed to the priesthood of all the faithful. Pastors then must recognize that their ministry is meant first of all for the service of the whole people of God. In their turn the laity must recognize that they need this ministry in order to share in the Church's mission' (article 22).

As for the calling to lay ministry, the more gospel-inspired laity there are, ready to engage in the world of politics, economics, the sciences and arts, as well as professional life, home life, and such things as education and even suffering, the more we are able to share in the building up of the Kingdom. It is one of our privileges to listen to the accounts by young men and women of the varied ways in which God has led them to offer themselves for particular forms of ministry. There is a variety of gifts, and the leadership needed today in the Church is not the kind which holds all the strings in one pair of hands.

We ourselves would wish to testify to the fulfilment of our calling – 'our duty and our joy'. Few vocations can be so stretching or provide so much opportunity for continuing growth. The call is for growth in holiness and in the service of those about us. There is significance in the Litany prayed at the ordination of a Roman Catholic bishop, priest or deacon:

Bless this chosen man.
Bless this chosen man and make him holy.
Bless this chosen man, make him holy and consecrate him for his sacred duties.

If asked what his ordination was for, the great men of this world might have hurried straight to 'his sacred duties'. But not so with the Church. The life and growth of a human being, the call to holiness, all come first if the busy task of the ordained minister is to produce the priest who will last. The same is true for the Christian with a sense of calling to his secular task. The same priorities hold for the lay Christian who quickly learns that the first calling by our Lord is to be with him. Retreat weeks, Quiet Days or Weekends, an early morning hour, or a half-day alone with our heavenly

Father, are as relevant and valuable to a busy consultant, politician or business man as to a bishop.

> *Loving Father, Lord of all the earth,*
> *we thank you for the variety of ministries*
> *to which you call your people*
> *for the service of mankind.*
> *Provide your Church, we pray,*
> *with the servants and the gifts she needs;*
> *help us all to listen to your voice,*
> *that we may readily do your will*
> *and complete the work you have for us.*
> *We ask this through Jesus Christ our Lord. Amen.*

Wednesday in Fifth Week of Lent
(John 8:31–42)

To the Jews who believed in him Jesus said:

'If you make my word your home
you will indeed be my disciples;
you will come to know the truth,
and the truth will set you free.'

They answered, 'We are descended from Abraham and we have never been the slaves of anyone; what do you mean, "You will be set free"?'
Jesus replied:

'In all truth I tell you,
everyone who commits sin is a slave . . .
. . . if the Son sets you free,
you will indeed be free.
I know that you are descended from Abraham;
but you want to kill me
because my word finds no place in you . . .
As it is, you want to kill me,
a man who has told you the truth
as I have learnt it from God;
that is not what Abraham did.
You are doing your father's work.'

They replied, 'We were not born illegitimate, the only father we have is God.' Jesus answered:

'If God were your father, you would love me,
since I have my origin in God and have come from him;
I did not come of my own accord,
but he sent me . . .'

John 8:31–34, 36–37, 40–42

The controversy becomes still more violent. They suggest that he was born illegitimate, hoping in this way to discredit him. Jesus responds, a little later on, by referring to their father as the devil (John 8:44). His mind probably went back to his confrontation with the devil in the wilderness: 'I will give you all these' kingdoms of the world and their splendour, 'if you fall at my feet and do me homage' (Matthew 4:9). How did it come about that those who loved the Law of God and spent so much time studying the scriptures, could become so hostile to Jesus that they planned together for his death, or at least went along with his public execution?

A brief explanation for some of them, at least, is that the Pharisees were making an heroic attempt to maintain the identity of Israel in a world where, amidst different faiths and philosophies, every kind of value easily became relative. Only the way of steadfast and rigid obedience could ensure that the Law was known and God's will truly accepted by a sinful nation. They saw the coming of Jesus and his way of life as a clear threat to all that patient work of teaching and enforcing the Law.

He, on the other hand, was calling into question the whole of their law-based approach to life. With him the great issues of life were not bounded by 'How shall we get by?' or 'How shall we avoid evil?' Rather, the question was 'What shall we live for?' They saw the coming of light into their world but were so trapped in the system of their making, and fearful of losing what they had established, that they called light darkness and did not allow the truth which he brought them, to penetrate their minds.

So he talked about their need for liberation: 'If you make my word your home . . . the truth will set you free . . . If the Son sets you free, you will indeed be free' (John 8:31, 32, 35).

For Christians who know oppression, the liberation of which Christ speaks is a great comfort. Inevitably they turn also to the Book of Exodus for the Old Testament account of the great moment of liberation, which set the people of Israel free from oppression to manage their own affairs. Liberation theology is sometimes mistakenly assumed to be arguing for violent revolution. In fact it is a method of theology which tries to look at the world from the viewpoint of the oppressed and of God's purpose for them.

It is of particular concern for Christians when the dominant group denying freedom of choice to whole peoples is made up of practising Christians. That is why South Africa is of such importance to the Church. We were invited to pay a visit last year by the two Archbishops of Cape Town, acting in the name of our Churches in Southern Africa. Because of the wide base our Churches have, we were able, in the course of our eighteen-day visit, to cross many of the barriers which divide South Africans so deeply. In addition to the local leaders of our Churches, we met Chairmen of international business concerns, Trade Union leaders, student groups, lawyers and groups of white church people. What most shaped our impressions was to visit more than a dozen black or coloured Townships: there we sometimes stayed overnight, visited people in their homes, saw a variety of projects, listened at length to those who live and work there. We had been told by sportsmen and business visitors that things were better, that Apartheid was crumbling and that the troubles had calmed down. We found that on the contrary the situation was more terrible than in advance we had imagined.

In inviting us, our bishops had told us how damaging was the effect of the State of Emergency's clampdown on news reporting, which was leading people to believe that there was no trouble. We quickly saw for ourselves the importance of our Lord's words: 'The truth shall set you free'. We were greatly encouraged by much that we saw of church life, standing and suffering with people in their struggle for freedom. We were impressed by the ability and maturity of so many of the Churches' black leaders, and by the vigour and joy of their worship. Amidst so much frustration and tension, we were humbled by the readiness to forgive, to go on working for a united South Africa and to use peaceful methods.

How does it come about that, while many white South African Christians are courageously committed to the struggle for justice, many others defend or tolerate the *status quo*? Because they have suppressed the truth, they believe their own propaganda, fed by the fear of losing their identity and the shape of society which their parents believed God had brought about. They totally overlook the benefits which could be brought to the country by the gifts and talents God has given to their black brothers and sisters.

What about Christians in our own country? When we look at our nation from the point of view of the poor, both black people and white people, and of God's purposes for them, we cannot be complacent about the priorities of our society. We too need to ask how our Lord wishes to set people free to make choices affecting their own lives. Even at the risk of becoming as unpopular as he did, we too must insist that the great issues of life are not bounded by 'How will we get by?' or 'How shall we avoid evil?' The question for us is 'What shall we live for?'

> *Our loving Lord, we thank you*
> *for the price you paid to set us free,*
> *and for the freedoms we experience*
> *to worship, to debate, to work and to learn.*
> *We pray for those denied their freedoms,*
> *and for those who knowingly or unknowingly are oppressors.*
> *Set them free from their fears*
> *and from the grip of unjust systems:*
> *we make this prayer through our Saviour, Jesus Christ.*

> *God bless Africa.*
> *Guard her children*
> *Guide her rulers*
> *and give her peace. Amen.*

Thursday in Fifth Week of Lent

(Psalm 104:4–9 [105:4–9])

> *Consider the Lord and his strength;*
> *constantly seek his face.*
> *Remember the wonders he has done,*
> *his miracles, the judgements he spoke.*

> *O children of Abraham, his servant,*
> *O sons of the Jacob he chose.*
> *He, the Lord, is our God:*
> *his judgements prevail in all the earth.*

> *He remembers his covenant for ever,*
> *his promise for a thousand generations,*
> *the covenant he made with Abraham,*
> *the oath he swore to Isaac.*
> **Psalm 104:4–9 [105:4–9]**

To emphasize the richness of the Scriptures set before us during Lent, we have chosen for today some verses from the Psalm given us as the link between the Old Testament Reading and the extract from the gospel. It is taken from the Grail version of the Psalms, a metrical translation to enable its easy recitation or singing aloud.

In the Psalms young people especially are put in mind of the goodness down the years of God who 'remembers his covenant for ever'. The stories of God's faithful dealings with Abraham, Isaac and Jacob, with Moses, Aaron and in the Exodus from Egypt, were rehearsed over and over again. The Psalms served in Israel, as they do for many Christians today, both for private prayer and for public worship. They put into words the experience of individuals, and also the story of whole communities.

Whenever we use a Psalm in prayers at home, in a broadcast service, in a great cathedral or with a monastic community, saying or singing them through the different hours of the day, the whole Church prays with us. With the Church around us, we are able to bring to God our personal struggles through the words of the Psalmist. St John Cassian, writing early in the fifth century, said: 'The good man will sing the Psalms no longer as verses composed by a prophet, but as born of his own prayers . . . When we use the words, we remember our own circumstances and struggles, the results of our negligence or earnestness, the mercies of God's providence or the temptations of the devil, the subtle and slippery sins of forgetfulness or human frailty or unthinking ignorance. All these feelings we find expressed in the Psalms.'

As we have seen earlier in Lent, the Psalmists cried to God with their prayers of protest at the injustices or sufferings they endured. They wrestled with these 'in the sanctuary of God', as they remembered his goodness to other generations. When our worship takes the form of constantly claiming victory over suffering and weakness, sensitive and hurt Christians today are denied this spiritual resource. Worship needs to strike a balance. It is of course the offering of whole-hearted praise, but it should also give space and stillness for us to raise our personal needs before God. It must somehow give opportunity for the Christian who in a hard world needs help in facing an active, mature and costly struggle.

When Jews, scattered around the world, celebrate the Passover, they say to one another, 'Next year in Jerusalem'. They continue to hold God's promise in front of them. The New Testament encourages Christians to do something very similar: the Kingdom of God, the city of God, the new Jerusalem, will come in completeness beyond this life. 'Faith *believes* in the last things,' wrote Dietrich Bonhoeffer, 'faith *does* the next to last things.' In the light of God's promise, what kind of people are we today? Do we tolerate contradictions to his promise? Such a dream of the future does not encourage us to withdraw from the struggle in the belief that there is nothing effective we can do now. It leads us to try to change the course of events wherever that is possible.

Young people respond to the inspiration of good dreams. Recently in a popular radio programme about Martin Luther King, a gospel choir did not hesitate to take up some of this theme in the idiom of modern gospel music, as some recordings were played of parts of his speeches — 'I have a dream', 'I've been up to the mountain', 'If there's nothing you would die for . . . ' The words seemed an appropriate challenge to young people, including his plea for equal opportunities for black children, his description of personal fear at one moment in face of threats, his trust in the promise of the Lord's presence; and 'Free at last, free at last'. Such dreams carry many of us with them. We know that there are many 'next to last things' to be done if we are to give these dreams reality.

Together with Merseyside Free Church representatives, we have led ecumenical youth pilgrimages to Taizé, Iona, Lindisfarne and Holy Island . . . and shortly to Assisi. We travel together in one large coach with some forty-five young people from different Churches, aged between 17 and 25. On the pilgrimage we see these young people passing through different stages: first enthusiasms give way to unease, as they learn more of the differences between Churches. Then friendships emerge and, with them, a growing understanding that true and sincere Christians are to be found in each of the Churches. Like the Psalmists, they and we can reflect on our histories, which, in those ancient Christian places to which we all have attachment, remind us that God 'keeps his covenant for ever'. Before long the young pilgrims challenge us with their impatience for unity, criticizing church structures and disciplines for worship. We do our best to explain all this to them and to encourage them to build on so much which they share already. Over the years we go on meeting some of them as they take up responsibilities, most of them lay, some now ordained. They bring with them a firm expectation that it is the normal way of working in church life for Christians to plan, learn and work together.

It is very healthy for bishops to hear their impatience, those normal expectations and their questions about the world. As we talk through these matters with them, many of them see that there needs to be a determined and long-term commitment, if the dreams they share with us are to become true. We are encouraged that the future of the Church is in such hands.

Lord, you have held the past in your hands:
we know that you hold the future in your hands.
Remember your covenant for ever.
As we pray for young people in our Churches,
we take heart from your faithfulness.
May they see with their eyes what we have longed for,
our church divisions healed and reconciled,
our dreams of justice fulfilled.
Lord, lead their impatience into urgency
and grant them the endurance to go with it.
We make this prayer through our faithful Lord,
even Jesus Christ. Amen.

Friday in Fifth Week of Lent

(Jeremiah 20:10–13)

I heard so many disparaging me,
'Terror on every side!
Denounce him! Let us denounce him!'
All those who were on good terms with me
watched for my downfall,
'Perhaps he will be seduced into error.
Then we shall get the better of him
and take our revenge!'
But Yahweh is at my side like a mighty hero;
my opponents will stumble, vanquished,
confounded by their failure;
everlasting, unforgettable disgrace will be theirs.
Yahweh Sabaoth, you who test the upright,
observer of motives and thoughts, I shall see your vengeance on them,
for I have revealed my cause to you.

Jeremiah 20:10–12

When people were discussing who Jesus was, one of the answers given was that he was Jeremiah or one of the prophets. At first sight, the idea of connecting Jesus with the prophet, who so often had to pronounce God's judgement on the people of God, seems most incongruous: until you look beneath the surface. More than any other figure in the Old Testament, Jeremiah has left behind him an account of the making of a soul. In what have sometimes been called 'The Confessions of Jeremiah' we are allowed a deep insight into the wrestling with God of a most sensitive person. Those who saw our Lord unashamedly weeping in public – and later in the agony and bloody sweat he endured in Gethsemane – recognized some of the same costly searching for the will of God in a very vulnerable person, not unlike the character of Jeremiah. In spite of the personal hurts which he reveals, his sense of God's presence endures: 'Yahweh is at my side like a mighty hero'. His faith is never the serene possession which we often assume ought to be true of the faithful believer.

Look, for example, at the complaining which we find side by side with spiritual resources in Jeremiah 15:10–21.

A disaster for me, mother, that you bore me
to be a man of strife and dissension for the whole country . . .
Have I not genuinely done my best to serve you, Yahweh? . . .
Yahweh, you know! . . .
Realise that I suffer insult for your sake.
When your words came, I devoured them:
Your word was my delight
and the joy of my heart . . .

We read here the words of someone who was bitterly hurt by the criticism and attacks made upon him. These came first from his own family, when he was accused of betraying the old ways of his priestly ancestors. Then came the shock for this country boy of seeing the reality of life in the holy city, Jerusalem. (His experience must have been not dissimilar from that of devout Christian West Indians, when they came to London, where the missionaries came from, in the 1950s.) Wherever Jeremiah looked, he found disloyalty to the God of Israel, immorality, injustice and lies.

At first he told himself that these sinners were only the poor who knew no better. He would approach the great men, who would know and observe the Law of the Lord. But it was no better there: 'they do not even know how to blush'. Their sophistication has removed every inhibition and sense of shame. Jeremiah's burning indignation bubbled over with God's judgement on the sinful nation. When the great power of Babylon came against Jerusalem, the government tried to rally the people with patriotic speeches. Jeremiah had the courage to say that God would not defend them, but would carry them away into exile. Not surprisingly he was denounced vehemently, and his life itself was endangered. It was out of those terrifying moments that his indignant prayers came, pleading with God to take vengeance on his enemies.

There is something almost shocking in Jeremiah's cry for vengeance. In a sense that shock is right, when we compare it with Jesus and his prayer for his enemies. But these uncensored prayers from an afflicted prophet have a challenge for us. The absence or control of anger when we are confronted with evil, can be a most alarming symptom. If we visit an old lady who has been 'mugged', or a parent whose child has been killed by a drunken driver who has been given only a derisory sentence, and we do not ourselves feel with such people a profound anger, something must be seriously wrong in us. It might well suggest that we do not really care about right and wrong. Far from being above such feelings of anger and vengeance, we would be beneath them. On the other hand it is sadly true that the higher a person's motives, the greater the danger that he or she becomes intolerant, condemnatory, fanatical. Such people become really dangerous in Church or state.

There are undoubtedly some Christians with 'one skin less' and whose feelings are much more raw to the touch than are others'. For them the experience and cry of Jeremiah can be quite helpful. Often such people are made to feel inferior, even guilty, that they do not possess the kind of calm peace of mind which seems to come naturally to their more thick-skinned sisters and brothers. Those sun-tanned and serene Christians have forgotten the great saints who went through the 'dark night of the soul', and whose feelings were much closer to the surface. 'She's too sensitive', 'They always seem to have a chip on their shoulders', or 'He should pull himself together' are comments which take no account of the insecurity which may be deep-rooted in someone else's experience. Such critics have no regard for persons who perhaps yearn for some form of loving support.

The more sensitive personalities will find far more help from unjudging acceptance in the body of Christ than if they are told to 'snap out of it'. Indeed, once we recognize that God accepts them as they are, with all that they are, it is we who receive remarkable insights through them – things of which we may previously have been quite unaware. Perhaps we, like the sophisticated rulers who confronted Jeremiah, have forgotten how to blush, or to be afraid, or even to be angry. The Christian way does include forgiving our enemies, but the prophet's prayers of protest show that in such an interchange with God our hearts can be healed and we can be changed. The story of sensitive Jeremiah is the story of the growth of a soul. For him to be so aware of his deep feelings allowed the Lord, his mighty hero, to go to work.

Father, you encourage us
to pour out our hearts to you in prayer,
as we become more aware of what we have become
through sweet or bitter experience.

May we help to make our part of your body
a place where the most wounded know they belong,
and where their insights will enrich all our growing.
Through Jesus Christ our Healer. Amen.

Saturday in Fifth Week of Lent

(John 11:45–57)

Then the chief priests and the Pharisees called a meeting. 'Here is this man
working all these signs,' they said, 'and what action are we taking? If we let
him go on in this way everybody will believe in him, and the Romans will
come and suppress the Holy Place and our nation.' One of them, Caiaphas,
the high priest that year, said, 'You do not seem to have grasped the
situation at all; you fail to see that it is to your advantage that one man
should die for the people, rather than that the whole nation should perish.'
He did not speak in his own person, but as high priest of that year he was
prophesying that Jesus was to die for the nation – and not for the nation
only, but also to gather together into one the scattered children of God. From
that day onwards they were determined to kill him.

John 11:47–53

The gloves are off now and any remaining pretence has vanished. The
power of those who are determined to kill Jesus is clear after this meeting of
the priests, with the military might of the Roman army of occupation behind
them. What kind of forces could be mustered on our Lord's side? He could
no longer move about openly; just the small band of his followers stood
with him. A hothead amongst them went out and purchased a sword or two.
Otherwise no outward preparations were made for the seemingly inevitable
struggle ahead. Yet Jesus was able to speak of a greater following than all
the princes in the world: 'When I am lifted up from the earth, I shall draw all
people to myself' (John 12:32). His disciples were to remember the harsh and
ruthless words of Caiaphas as having more truth than he had realized when
he spoke them. Jesus was indeed 'to die for the nation – and not for the
nation only, but also to gather together into one the scattered children of
God' (John 11:51–52).

At various stages of this Lenten journey together, we have asked ourselves what kind of God do we believe in and worship. We ask that question
again and again as we follow our Lord through Holy Week and to the heart

of our salvation. As we repeat this key question, we realize that many of us today have ideas about God which we have received from somewhere else than the gospels. Some may well have prejudices which are not drawn from the God we see revealed in Jesus Christ. As we try to analyse them, we begin to understand a little better the prejudices of Caiaphas the high priest and his followers. For instance, there are those who claim that God can do whatever he wants like a very powerful ruler. Moreover he has vast forces on whom he can call at any moment. Then there are those who believe that the Lord protects and prospers his friends or that he is the God of *our* fathers and of *our* nation. Others assume that he makes harsh judgements about you if you do not fit in with the way of his Church. We grow with ready-made ideas like these which we have picked up from various sources and experiences. How will they stand up to the account we receive as we follow Jesus through the agony of Holy Week to Easter?

What of the all-powerful, protective God, prospering his friends? Last Good Friday, together with Doctor John Newton, Merseyside's Free Church Moderator, both of us went out to make the Stations of the Cross in a perimeter estate outside Liverpool. The closure of a large factory there had been announced a week or two before. As on a number of similar occasions during our years in Liverpool, we had talked with both the management of the factory and the shop stewards in the hope that some way forward might be found in an area where there was already 30 per cent unemployment. As is frequently the case, the decision had really been firmly made some while before the announcement of the closure. Often our only hope is that whatever protest we may make may help to discourage any other firm from taking a similar decision.

As we mentioned to a very experienced priest, walking with his people along his sad route of prayerful protest and solidarity that afternoon, there was little we could hope to achieve except reasonable redundancy terms. He smiled kindly, and just said, 'I know. All we are trying to do is to help these people, who are losing their jobs, to relate their suffering to Calvary.' The God and Father of the Jesus of Holy Week is not a God who offers miraculous protection and special treatment. Rather, he suffers with us and draws those who recognize the love which stems from the cross to follow him on the route to the Easter Garden. It is when we keep our eyes on that destination that we are able to recognize what kind of protection he does offer on the way of the cross.

The understanding that he is the God of our fathers, of our nation, also takes some knocks, except in the strange way that the prophecy of Caiaphas worked out. The rift with the powerful leaders of the nation meant that there was no possibility of what might be called a 'top-down' movement to follow Jesus' way. Whole-hearted Christian discipleship has often led to unpopularity with the powers that be. And yet his following becomes much more than just a nation. We are members of an international movement, embracing nearly two thousand years, and reaching across all barriers of race and class. Jesus died 'not for the nation only, but to gather together in unity the scattered children of God'. As we regard the history of the Church, it is evident that more often than not, membership has grown from the 'bottom-up', from the humble and poor rather than by influence in the first instance from noble families.

Many people still seem to believe that the judgement of God is against them if they do not fit in with what they regard as the ways of the Church. Some people, who believe this, have found to their surprise that, even though certain religious people seem to disapprove of them and their way of life, the suffering Christ understands the feelings in their heart. Wilfred Owen wrote a preface to one of his War Poems in which a young man is blaspheming as he dies: 'There is a point where prayer is indistinguishable from blasphemy. There is also a point where blasphemy is indistinguishable from prayer.' Somehow we know that the God of Holy Week encourages prayers which express what we really feel rather than what we think we ought to feel.

As we approach Holy Week, it is our prayer that some people who at this time are feeling the hurt of failure, loss or death, may look with newly sensitive eyes as the story of the suffering, death and rising again of Jesus unfolds this year.

Lord Jesus,
you faced the deadly enmity of great forces:
your weapons were self-sacrifice and love.
We thank you for all the scattered children of God
gathered together in unity by your love.
Hear the prayers of those who cry out in anguish,
however they may cry: for you understand,
our Saviour and our God. Amen.

Group material

Starting points

- Recall the portrait of Jeremiah from Friday's Reading and reflection.
- Do his story and his deep feelings remind you of anyone?
- What can we learn from him about prayer?

Deeper reflection

1. A central theme of this week's readings is life and the gifts and demands of being fully alive.
   - What, during this past week, has made you feel more alive?
   - When has life ever felt to you like an adventure?
   - What are the things that diminish or deaden life?

2. On Tuesday we reflected on our need for holiness of life, whatever our different callings.
   - What does holiness of life mean to you?
   - How does your calling help you to grow in holiness?

3. God's purpose is liberation for everyone. Yet there are many in our world who are not free – not just the black people in South Africa but here in our own society.
   - How can we look at our society from the viewpoint of those who are poor or oppressed? What do we see?

4. As we enter Holy Week, we can consider where we stand now.
   - What kind of God have we discovered in this Lenten journey so far?

Prayer

Look back at the lines from Psalm 104 [105] which we read on Thursday. Read them very slowly with time for prayer.

Turn then to the Holy Spirit and ask that the Spirit will kindle our senses during the days of Holy Week and Easter so that we may live them to the full.

Say a prayer to the Holy Spirit.

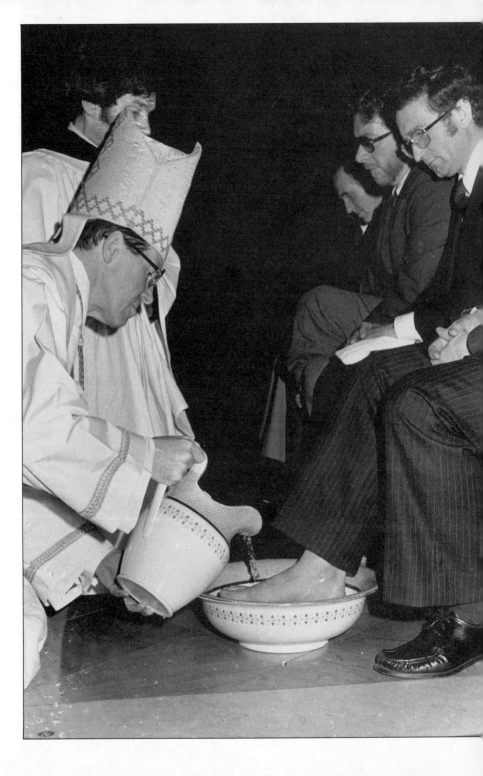

HOLY WEEK

'For us such a "ministry of the towel" is not a duty carried out in subservience. It must be a reflection of and response to the love of our servant Lord. Our imitation of his example, however inadequate we may be, must be given in a Christ-like manner.'

Page 150

Archbishop Derek carries out the washing of the feet ceremony on Maundy Thursday, Metropolitan Cathedral, Liverpool.

Palm Sunday
(Matthew 21:1–11)

When they were near Jerusalem and had come to Bethphage on the Mount of Olives, then Jesus sent two disciples, saying to them, 'Go to the village facing you, and you will at once find a tethered donkey and a colt with her. Untie them and bring them to me. If anyone says anything to you, you are to say, "The Master needs them and will send them back at once".' This was to fulfil what was spoken by the prophet:

Say to the daughter of Zion:
Look, your king is approaching,
humble and riding on a donkey
and on a colt, the foal of a beast of burden.

So the disciples went and did as Jesus had told them. They brought the donkey and the colt . . . and he took his seat on them. Great crowds of people spread their cloaks on the road, while others were cutting branches from the trees and spreading them in his path. The crowds who went in front of him and those who followed were all shouting:

Hosanna to the son of David!
Blessed is he who is coming in the name of the Lord!
Hosanna in the highest heavens!

And when he entered Jerusalem, the whole city was in turmoil as people asked, 'Who is this?' and the crowds answered, 'This is the prophet Jesus from Nazareth in Galilee.'

Matthew 21:1–11

Today sees the beginning of Holy Week, during which we try to stay with Jesus from the moment of his entry into Jerusalem, to his abandonment in Gethsemane, his lonely agony on Golgotha, to the tomb and the glory of his Resurrection. All this is encompassed in our remembrance and prayers of the next eight days. Nowadays it is customary to hear the four gospel accounts of our Lord's suffering, or the Passion as we call them, in the course of Holy Week. So we have thought it best to start with the verses which are often read today before a group of Christians sets out for a Palm Sunday procession. In these verses St Matthew describes the entry of Jesus into the holy city of Jerusalem, almost as a sign of his coming into his Kingdom. For the procession is not only a sign of our commitment to try to follow Jesus faithfully, especially during these days of Holy Week; it is also the expression of our belief that in going to his death, he is returning in glory to his Father, his mission of redemption complete.

It was soon evident, early that Sunday morning, when Jesus set out for Bethany, that a number of enthusiasts had gathered there, intensely curious about what had happened to Lazarus only a short time before. Some of the crowd will of course have been Galileans, en route to the celebration of the Passover. Others had undoubtedly come out from Jerusalem to check on the rumours which were still flying around about the raising of Lazarus from the dead. With luck, they would not only see Jesus and what challenge he might make to the authorities; they might even catch a glimpse of the man he had restored to life. Apparently it was customary for some of the people of Jerusalem to go out to meet large and important groups of pilgrims coming for the Passover feast, and to bring them, amidst singing, into the holy city. So excitement was high.

For Jesus and his disciples it represented a certain change in tactic. Normally, at such a time the Master kept a low profile. But on this occasion, as he neared Bethphage, on the outskirts of Jerusalem, he sent two of the disciples ahead, probably to a friend's house, to find a donkey, an untrained colt, upon which he would make what by that time was clearly going to be a triumphal entry. To us a donkey-ride may make us think of children on the sands at the seaside. But it seems that for the Jewish people a donkey or mule was regarded as a very suitable mount for a ritual occasion. The humility of our Lord's gesture, which appeals to us so much today, was not necessarily what appealed to the crowd, including a large number of Jewish children, all of whom seem to have delighted in this celebration.

In his gospel, Matthew is evidently anxious to recall the messianic prophecy of the past: 'Look, your king is approaching . . . humble and riding on a donkey and on a colt, the foal of a donkey' (Zechariah 9:9). The crowd may have been sufficiently excited to make a triumph out of the humble entry into Jerusalem; but the real significance must surely have been once again the insistence of Jesus upon what kind of servant/king he had set out to be. Beyond all the hosannas which rang out in welcome and seeming recognition, it was the Christ of the temptations and the wilderness who was being acclaimed for the unpretentious, peace-loving, non-violent manner in which he was approaching the fulfilment of his saving mission.

That Jesus was indeed acclaimed is made plain by the evangelist: 'The whole city was in turmoil as people asked, "Who is this?" and the crowds answered, "This is the prophet Jesus from Nazareth in Galilee"' (Matthew 21:10–11). What happened must have made the priests and scribes even more anxious and determined to carry out their plan against his life. Sadly they found a willing instrument in Judas Iscariot, who was prepared to sell his master for thirty pieces of silver.

It is impossible not to notice the treachery of the crowd, willing to fête Jesus on his arrival, yet content only days later to call for his blood. At best it was fickle ignorance. When it came to his fellow Galileans and friends, their abandonment and rejection of him only days later was betrayal and cowardice beyond contempt. Undoubtedly some of the crowd will have gone along with the rest because they knew no better. But there will have been many willing to go along with the condemnation of Jesus simply because of the pressure of the opinion of those all about them.

Going along with the crowd is not always a physical movement. It is a surrender of personal responsibility to others whose fear or prejudice or plain hatred will dictate the nature of the judgement. Centuries later it is hard to see how anyone could have gone along with the crowd in demanding the death of Jesus. There is every reason to believe that, amongst those who called for his blood, were some of those whose hosannas had rung out during his triumphal entry into the holy city at the beginning of that week.

There will have been many occasions in the lives of all of us when we have gone along with the crowd, giving our assent to a doubtful or wrong decision because of fear, or ignorance, or desire to be on the winning side. Wanting to be 'in the crowd' is a heavy pressure on young people, which leads many to keep silent when the loudest voices are telling lies about another individual or group. Such pressures have to be faced by adults too; there are times when, as a matter of conscience, an MP or a councillor, for example, may have to refuse the Party whip in order to preserve his integrity, sometimes at considerable cost to his political career. But the pressure of the call to solidarity, and the popularity of public opinion, can also be persuasive forces. At other times there is fear, or the ability to persuade oneself that the matter is of no real consequence, that others know better.

We are called to follow Christ on his way to crucifixion between two thieves. That is fidelity. In praise of Christ we will go along with the crowd of Palm Sunday. We must be on our guard lest we get caught up in the crowd mocking him as he hangs on Calvary, crucified by our easy consent to the verdict sought by Pilate.

Father of mercies,
you have given us an example of humble and unselfish love in the sufferings
of your Son, Jesus.
Help us to bear witness to your truth at all times,
especially when we are under pressure to bow to untruth and injustice;

so that strengthened by mutual support,
we may enter together the heavenly Jerusalem.
We ask this through Jesus Christ our Lord. Amen.

Monday in Holy Week
(John 12:1–11)

Six days before the Passover, Jesus went to Bethany, where Lazarus was,
whom he had raised from the dead. They gave a dinner for him there;
Martha waited on them and Lazarus was among those at table. Mary
brought in a pound of very costly ointment, pure nard, and with it anointed
the feet of Jesus, wiping them with her hair; the house was filled with the
scent of the ointment. Then Judas Iscariot – one of his disciples, the man who
was to betray him – said, 'Why was this ointment not sold for three hundred
denarii and the money given to the poor?' . . . Jesus said, 'Leave her alone; let
her keep it for the day of my burial. You have the poor with you always,
you will not always have me.'

John 12:1–5, 7–8

The Reading chosen for today tells of an episode which occurred the night before Jesus set out with his disciples for Jerusalem. It is, as it were, the evening before Palm Sunday. He had returned from Jericho to his friends in Bethany, with whom to rest a little before going on to Jerusalem. Evidently a meal was being provided for him and his disciples, probably to a great extent in thanksgiving for the restoration of Lazarus to life. Once more our Lord more than matched with love the devoted care shown to him by Mary, who soothed his feet with precious ointment. The whole occasion was a welcome reassurance for his disciples amidst their growing realization of the mounting tension as they prepared to go with him to Jerusalem. But not for all of them. Judas Iscariot is shown up as one whose values are still not attuned to the generosity and warmth of his Master. The difference and seeming clash with Judas are just a foretaste of the personal tragedy which is to overtake him.

Holy Week brings us quickly face to face with the threatened rejection of Jesus and cruel violence. The power of evil is, as the days go by, revealed with ruthlessness and brutality beyond anything we could have expected. As we follow the account in the gospels, the threat and the reality divide even the followers of Jesus. People whom you would expect to stand rock solid in face of any challenge, deny their Lord. Those who have been happy enough to follow around as observers, melt quickly away as soon as the going becomes rough. On the other hand unexpected people, mainly women, find that their love for Jesus keeps them going despite the ugliness of developments. It is this which allows them somehow to manage their fears.

The members of the family at Bethany were amongst those who, despite the evidence of the growing hostility of the authorities, had maintained their loving friendship with Jesus and the disciples. They continued to offer their home to him as a place of welcome, refuge and support. It seems that it was there that he stayed on the Sabbath and then that evening the meal took place – so St Matthew tells us – at the house of a man called Simon, known as the leper from the skin-disease which afflicted him. It seems clear that he was a wealthy neighbour of the family: possibly Jesus had helped him at some time.

Lazarus himself must certainly have been amongst the guests, and his sister, the good housewife Martha, seems to have been responsible for directing affairs at the meal, in all probability waiting on Jesus and the others. Mary, the more reserved, kept in the background in the early stages but she must have put her resources together to show her devotion to Jesus. It was customary for guests to recline on divans so that their heads were towards the table and their feet away from it. At a certain point Mary entered, approached where Jesus was reclining and having anointed his feet with the highly-scented nard, proceeded to dry them off with her hair. It is this expensive, if not extravagant, gesture to which Judas takes exception. It may have cost a sizeable sum of money but Jesus defends Mary in this humble expression of her devotion.

It was this sort of devotion and commitment – what today we might call 'spoiling' – which marked out the attitude of this Bethany family towards Jesus. The closeness of such a bond explains why Jesus wept when he came to them on the death of Lazarus. We can understand just what such a refuge with close friends must have meant to him as a place for withdrawal.

Today the members of such a devoted group might easily be accused themselves of withdrawing from the harsh realities of life around them. Indeed that is the sort of charge occasionally laid at the door of religious women and Sisters, who are thought of as yielding to the temptation of steering clear of the conflicts which confront others. It is wrong to generalize. While some religious will justify themselves by stressing the prior importance of their worship of God, we have frequent evidence of the service which a withdrawn or enclosed community can give in its prayerful concern and help for those busily engaged elsewhere. For Jesus the support of the family at Bethany was a great strength and consolation; but it did not weaken his resolve to carry through the plan for the salvation of the world.

As for the expensive ointment and scent, there are always critics of many forms of expenditure in the cause of religion, especially any costly commitment to making beautiful buildings or aids to worship. They say that the money could better have been given to the poor. Both of us devote a good deal of energy to trying to find money and other resources for disadvantaged and poor people today. But devotion to the Lord, and beauty to assist in our worship of him, often provide the motivation which encourages people, in face of inevitable disappointments, to sustain their service alongside the poor.

Some years ago a young man was working himself into the ground in voluntary work with homeless people on London's Embankment. The clergyman who was responsible for this work knew that the young man loved beautiful objects and took him for a day off, right away from the pressing demands of the riverside. They went together to the Ashmolean Museum in Oxford. He saw the young man admiring a jewelled chalice and asked him, 'Which do you think is the more valuable, this chalice or the plastic cups we use to offer a drink to the homeless on the Embankment?' Unhesitatingly the reply came: 'The chalice is the more valuable, because beautiful worship prompts that sort of service to the needy'.

If our worship is to offer the kind of temporary withdrawal which inspires service, we need consciously to hold together that integral relationship which unites prayer with the service we carry out in Christ's name. So we bring our anxieties to the altar, just as we bring the gospel to our service with and for the community.

At a weekend conference recently, Christian youth leaders were encouraged at the act of worship on the first evening to take a stone from buckets which were passed round: the stone would represent a burden which they had brought with them. It was suggested that they lay it aside for the weekend. During a period of quiet reflection, one by one, many of them laid their stone down on the floor in the middle of the room, and in such a way as to form one large cross. During another service at the end of the weekend, they were encouraged to pick up the burdens they had laid aside, praying that they might be able to do so with fresh attitudes as a result of that weekend of withdrawal and prayer. Our prayer is that, whatever withrawal you may plan for the rest of this week, you may recognize the cross in your burden and be able to keep going, even when the way is stony for you.

We worship and thank you, Lord Jesus,
for your unswerving love for us.
May our times of reflection, prayer and study
inspire us to persevere in service
alongside your other needy ones.
We ask this of you, Lord,
who laid down your life for us. Amen.

Tuesday in Holy Week

(John 13:21–33, 36–38)

Having said this, Jesus was deeply disturbed and declared, 'In all truth I tell you, one of you is going to betray me.' The disciples looked at each other, wondering whom he meant. The disciple Jesus loved was reclining next to Jesus; Simon Peter signed to him and said, 'Ask who it is he means,' so leaning back close to Jesus' chest he said, 'Who is it, Lord?' Jesus answered, 'It is the one to whom I give the piece of bread that I dip in the dish.' And when he had dipped the piece of bread he gave it to Judas son of Simon Iscariot. At that instant, after Judas had taken the bread, Satan entered him. Jesus then said, 'What you are going to do, do quickly' . . . When he had gone, Jesus said:

'Now has the Son of God been glorified,
and in him God has been glorified . . .
Little children,
I shall be with you only a little longer.
You will look for me,
and, as I told the Jews,
where I am going,
you cannot come . . .'

Simon Peter said, 'Lord, where are you going?' Jesus replied, 'Now you cannot follow me where I am going, but later you shall follow me.' Peter said to him, 'Why can I not follow you now? I will lay down my life for you.' 'Lay down your life for me?' answered Jesus. 'In all truth I tell you, before the cock crows you will have disowned me three times.'

John 13:21–27, 31, 33, 36–38

Tomorrow – Spy Wednesday as it is sometimes called because it seems to have been on that day that Judas Iscariot went to the chief priests and sold his Master for thirty pieces of silver – we are given St Matthew's account of the betrayal. Today the same sad picture is given to us by the beloved disciple John. It is the account of the one who was able to lean back so close to Jesus' chest that they could have a whispered exchange. They were reclining by the supper-table, just as we have described for the meal at Bethany. But it remains a mystery as to why, if he was able to identify the one whom Jesus indicated as his betrayer, John seems to have done nothing to stop Judas.

Perhaps our Lord also indicated to his young friend that he should treat the information confidentially. More likely he was persuaded by the impression gained by the other disciples that Jesus had merely told Judas, who was in charge of the common purse, to go and buy some provisions to see them over the festival. Or it could have been that Judas had been dispatched to give some money to the poor. We may be quite sure that in the long night watches later in the week, John must often have asked himself why he did nothing at that critical moment. It can really only have been because of John's supreme confidence in Jesus' handling of the question he had put on Peter's behalf: in any case such treachery amongst friends was unthinkable. It is at least as idle to make too detailed an examination of Judas Iscariot's motive. All sorts of fanciful reasons are offered, from avarice to his possible disillusion about the kind of Kingdom this gentle, compassionate prophet was about to set up; certainly not Judas' idea of a real messiah. Whatever triggered off the final decision to break with Jesus and his fellow disciples, it was the result of a gradual process of disenchantment, not an act on the spur of the moment. When later on the horror of what he had done began to break over him, Judas fell victim to terrible despair.

St John's gospel account provides some contrast to this, with the reaction by Simon Peter to the suggestion that the enemies of Jesus might yet succeed in frustrating the Master's plan. The disciples must have realized that the hour of which the Lord had spoken had indeed come, fraught with danger. If there was to be an arrest, it was almost certain that the attempt to kill or capture must be before the celebration of the festival began. The crowds who had turned out the previous Sunday to welcome them into Jerusalem must have been reassuring. This, with his natural confidence, was enough to lead Peter himself into the real danger-spot. He would not allow anyone to lay a hand on Jesus. He, Peter, would personally defend Jesus, to the point of death, if need be. He must have been shaken as well as angered with our Lord's rejoinder 'Before the cock crows you will have disowned me three times'. Pride comes before the fall.

We have said of Judas that his decision to betray Jesus was not taken on the spur of the moment. Some jealousy and frustration, perhaps indignation at apparent rejection of advice, must have been smouldering within him. Probably finding no audience amongst the other disciples for his complaints, he will have stored up his grievances until they exploded, and he felt he could take no more. Not so Simon Peter, brought low in this first instance by an impetuous outburst of over-confidence in his ability to shake off the attacks of others upon the reputation of his Master. Beyond doubt there was more than a streak of impetuosity in his character. It fed his leadership, acknowledged by Jesus. But when that impetuous expression of confidence was based on himself rather than the Jesus he loved, his strength of character was undermined.

Those who must bear the burden of responsibility must always be on their guard lest they be overtaken by pride, or even by that confidence in self which experience of office can build up over the years. We are never more susceptible to temptation than when we think we are beyond its reach and have a particular weakness, of which we are aware, well under control if not actually beaten. There is something of Peter in all of us who must give the service of authority.

> Lord Jesus,
> save us from over-confidence or despair.
> It is only because you are our Lord
> that we may presume to show the way to others.
> Help us lest we stumble
> over our own self-importance;
> and when we trip over our own feet,
> give us the humble faith to get up and go on.
> Through the same Christ our Lord. Amen.

Wednesday in Holy Week

(Matthew 26:14–25)

Then one of the Twelve, the man called Judas Iscariot, went to the chief priests and said, 'What are you prepared to give me if I hand him over to you?' They paid him thirty silver pieces, and from then onwards he began to look for an opportunity to betray him.

Now on the first day of Unleavened Bread the disciples came to Jesus to say, 'Where do you want us to make the preparations for you to eat the Passover?' He said, 'Go to a certain man in the city and say to him, "The Master says: My time is near. It is at your house that I am keeping Passover with my disciples."' The disciples did what Jesus told them and prepared the Passover.

When evening came he was at table with the Twelve. And while they were eating he said, 'In truth I tell you, one of you is about to betray me.' They were greatly distressed and started asking him in turn, 'Not me, Lord, surely?' He answered, 'Someone who has dipped his hand into the dish with me will betray me. The Son of man is going to his fate, as the scriptures say he will, but alas for that man by whom the Son of man is betrayed! Better for that man if he had never been born!' Judas, who was to betray him, asked in his turn, 'Not me, Rabbi, surely?' Jesus answered, 'It is you who say it.'

Matthew 26:14–25

Here is St Matthew's account of the same episode which St John recorded for us yesterday, though with this difference. Yesterday, from the viewpoint of the beloved disciple John, we heard first of the exchange with Judas and then the warning to Peter. Today we hear of all the disciples in turn responding to the Lord's charge that one of his friends would betray him. 'Not me, Lord, surely?' The mind of Judas was already made up. The preliminary deal with the chief priests had already been done. Therefore the repetition by Judas of that innocent clearing question can only have been to see if suspicions in his regard were already aroused, and to throw the other disciples off the scent. To Judas the answer was, 'It is you who say it'. To him it can only have meant, 'You know the answer to that yourself'.

It mattered very much to Jesus to face the crisis with all his friends and disciples around him. As the account proceeds, we see him eventually standing quite alone; but that was not his wish. We see how carefully he has laid plans for the Passover supper with his twelve apostles. When he goes into the garden of Gethsemane to pray, he takes his inner circle of three – Peter and the two sons of Zebedee, James and John – with him. The solidarity of the Twelve was very important to him, and his betrayal by one of them must indeed have felt like a stab in the back.

All that took place had in fact been foretold in the Scriptures. That does not mean that Judas was chosen as an apostle so that inevitably he might fit the role of the one to betray his Master. To claim that would be to deny his freedom of will. But his decision, freely made, was foreseen in the eternal 'now' whence the Scriptures were inspired. Presumably Judas was selected by Jesus because of his gifts, as somebody who potentially might be a good apostle. It was his responsibility when he chose to turn his back on the grace and truth he saw in Jesus.

In our own country especially, people often feel that ideally Christians should stand on their own two feet, bearing their own burdens, perhaps with stiff upper lips as well. The way of Christian maturity in which Jesus was leading his apostles was not towards independence as individuals but towards interdependence. The picture of the 'perfect Man fully mature with the fullness of Christ himself' (Ephesians 4:13) focusses on the growth of Christians together in the body of Christ, 'every joint adding its own strength, for each individual part to work according to its function. So the body grows until it has built itself up in love' (Ephesians 4:16). As bishops, we probably know most of the damaging things which can be said about the Church; for people send for bishops when something really bad or difficult has happened. Nevertheless both of us would testify that the longer we live, the more conscious we are of the strength of the body of Christ, the support we receive from it, and the variety of gifts it encompasses.

Liverpool's history has known more than its fair share of economic depression and disasters. Strong expressions of solidarity – in family, parish and neighbourhood – have been an important factor in helping people to survive these hard experiences. Of course, there are also negative aspects to solidarity which can produce at local level a sort of tribalism which distrusts all others and defends 'our own, right or wrong'. But the strength of belonging to a community, marked by true solidarity, is a great strength at a time of stress or sorrow.

Soon after last year's Hillsborough football disaster, a lecturer in the University went up to a colleague and gave her a hug. He said, 'I've decided to show people how much I value them while they're still alive, not wait till they're dead and then tell other people how much I valued them.' We realize that there are many who will say, 'We're not the hugging kind!' But it is possible to show people that we value them in many different ways: calling round to say 'hello' when we know that someone is going through a hard time, going for a walk with such a person, sitting and listening with one's full attention switched on. You might like to write to someone today whom you know is alone and anxious. Holiday postcards are fine, but it is times of stress which call for understanding and support. It has meant much to each of us, when there has been a personal attack or misrepresentation in the media, to receive a prompt call from the other.

True loyalty includes honest criticism, but there is all the difference in the world between contemptuously dismissing what 'they' have been doing, and honest positive criticism of what a sister or brother has been attempting.

The prophets of the Old Testament criticized what they loved. Such challenges can be received quite differently from those which have the feel of an outsider glorying in how badly they think the Church is tackling a task. 'Speaking the truth in love' (Ephesians 4:15 RSV) is one of the ways in which the body of Christ is helped to grow. For us, Christian discipleship has led to a liberating experience, along with the strength of knowing that we belong to the body of Christ. But the conscientious response to our Lord's 'It is you who say it' must be more than lip-service.

> Holy Spirit of God
> look in love on the Church,
> seeking to serve you in all the world.
> Turn her outwards from self-interest:
> heal her divisions,
> strengthen her pursuit of truth and love.
> Save each of us from holding back
> the generous self-giving which is asked of us:
> through Jesus Christ our Lord. Amen.

Maundy Thursday

(John 13:1–15)

They were at supper, and the devil had already put it into the mind of Judas Iscariot, son of Simon, to betray him. Jesus knew that the Father had put everything into his hands, and that he had come from God and was returning to God, and he got up from table, removed his outer garments and, taking a towel, wrapped it round his waist; he then poured water into a basin and began to wash the disciples' feet and to wipe them with the towel he was wearing.

He came to Simon Peter, who said to him, 'Lord, are you going to wash my feet?' Jesus answered, 'At the moment you do not know what I am doing, but later you will understand.' 'Never!' said Peter, 'You shall never wash my feet.' Jesus replied, 'If I do not wash you, you can have no share with me.' Simon Peter said, 'Well then, Lord, not only my feet, but my hands and my head as well!' Jesus said, 'No one who has had a bath needs washing, such a person is clean all over. You too are clean, though not all of you are' . . . When he had washed their feet and put on his outer garments again he went back to the table. 'Do you understand', he said, 'what I have done to you?

You call me Master and Lord, and rightly; so I am. If I, then, the Lord and Master, have washed your feet, you must wash each other's feet. I have given you an example so that you may copy what I have done to you.'

John 13:2–10, 12–15

Holy Thursday is in every sense a commemoration of our Lord Jesus Christ. When before supper he washed the feet of his disciples, he told them that he had given them an example so that they might copy what he had done to them. At supper itself, when he instituted the eucharist, blessing bread and wine and offering them to his friends as his body and blood, again he instructed them to 'do this in memory of me'.

At the Last Supper Jesus will have acted as head of the family, with the apostles reclining on divans arranged in a circle around the table, probably with Peter at one side of him and John at the other. In a sense one would be almost surprised if there was not some competition as to what positions the others were to occupy. Luke places after the meal words which were probably an echo of an earlier dispute: 'An argument also began between them about who should be reckoned the greatest' (Luke 22:24). John's version seems almost to suggest that it may have been occasioned by the attitude of Judas (John 13:2–5). At all events Jesus saw that some practical expression must now be given to all his earlier exhortations to humility.

So he rose from the table, laid aside his garments and girded himself with a towel. Then he set about the task normally associated with a servant. Welcome as this service must have been to those tired disciples, dusty and weary from their journey, Peter's protest was probably the expression of feelings widely felt amongst them. The humility of Jesus led inevitably to the humiliation of his friends. Even Judas had his feet washed, and by his Master who knew full well the treachery which was planned. It was on the part of Jesus a highly meaningful act of love, as was the institution of the eucharist at the end of the meal which followed.

The link between this infinitely powerful sacramental action and the foot-washing is not accidental. 'The ministry of the towel', as it is known to many, reflects perfectly the humility and love of the suffering Servant who is Redeemer of mankind.

'Do you understand what I have done to you?' Jesus asked his disciples, as he came back to the table and took his place in their midst. For us such a 'ministry of the towel' is not a duty carried out in subservience. It must be a reflection of and response to the love of our servant Lord. Our imitation of his example, however inadequate we may be, must be given in a Christ-like manner.

To be a servant still requires a certain resilience. To be willing to soak up criticism and almost inevitable misrepresentation calls for courage. It can take courage to remain silent in self-defence, when explanation can only be offered at the expense of others. This is where mutual trust between friends, especially on an ecumenical basis, can be a great help. It can also take courage to be forthright, when a 'no comment' may bring welcome disinterest. Christ chose to be silent before Pilate but he did not throw in the towel amongst the money-lenders in the Temple. There is nothing obsequious about such ministry. It is patient. It is kind. It envies no one and does not take offence. It is virile. It is compassionate. It is Christian.

It seems probable that, when the Lord's Supper had ended, the company lingered for a while. Judas had gone out into the night and Simon Peter had received his warning. It is then, according to St John, that Jesus delivers the long discourse with the commandment to love and the priestly prayer, emphasizing the mission of his disciples towards a hostile world which has rejected him. When at last Jesus moves to go on to Gethsemane, his friends must have been aware of pending difficulties, if not disaster. But there will have been few people around as they move outside. Most will have been at home with their families.

When Jesus and the disciples reached the garden, most of them will have gathered their cloaks about them, and settled down for the night. But he took with him the three who were closest to him and who had witnessed the transfiguration. Now as they dozed in and out of sleep they will have witnessed the bloody sweat upon Jesus as he agonized about what was to befall him. 'Then he said to them, "My soul is sorrowful to the point of death. Wait here and stay awake with me." And going on a little further he fell on his face and prayed. "My Father," he said, "if it is possible, let this cup pass me by. Nevertheless, let it be as you, not I, would have it"' (Matthew 26: 38–39). The scene for the agony and passion of our Lord is set.

Lord Jesus,
as you agonize and pray this night,
forgive us our weary neglect
of all those in need
whose wants we do not recognize.
Give us watchful eyes
to discover the beauty of your face,
hidden beneath the world's sorrow.
Help us to be the hands of your compassion
and a sign of your love.
Through the same Christ our Lord. Amen.

Good Friday
(John 18:1–19: 42)

They then took charge of Jesus, and carrying his own cross he went out to the Place of the Skull or, as it is called in Hebrew, Golgotha, where they crucified him with two others, one on either side, Jesus being in the middle . . . Near the cross of Jesus stood his mother and his mother's sister, Mary the wife of Clopas, and Mary of Magdala. Seeing his mother and the disciple whom he loved standing near her, Jesus said to his mother, 'Woman, this is your son.' Then to the disciple he said, 'This is your mother.' And from that hour the disciple took her into his home.

After this, Jesus knew that everything had now been completed and, so that the scripture should be completely fulfilled, he said: I am thirsty. A jar full of sour wine stood there; so, putting a sponge soaked in the wine on a hyssop stick, they held it up to his mouth. After Jesus had taken the wine he said, 'It is fulfilled'; and bowing his head he gave up his spirit.

John 19:17–18, 25–30

We hope that you may find it possible today to take time to read the whole long story of Christ's Passion, of which this is only an extract. You may like to compare the account given by John with that according to St Mark – or St Matthew or St Luke, for that matter. It is interesting to see the particular aspects of our Lord's sufferings which they stressed.

St Mark emphasizes the complete forsakenness and total rejection of Jesus: nothing relieves the weakness he experiences, the agony, the darkness. He describes how someone had to be pressed into helping Jesus to carry his cross; he is mocked by the passers-by, by the chief priests and even by the other condemned men hanging beside him. Darkness descends upon the land for three hours, and out of the darkness comes that terrible cry, 'My God, my God, why have you forsaken me?' He enters the darkest of all tunnels, the spiritual desolation of his soul, and goes down it as far as the furthest sinner is from God, so that no one is beyond the reach of his love. Even after that, the grim mocking continues. Someone takes up his word for God, 'Eloi', and says, 'Listen, he is calling on Elijah'. Another bystander, giving him the vinegar on the sponge, cries 'Wait! And see if Elijah will come to take him down'.

It is a vivid account of acute suffering. On the other hand St John is like a painter, perhaps Rembrandt, who concentrates all the light and the attention on one part of his picture. He allows the rest to blur, and form a background to the subject where his interest lies. He removes or obscures all the other details which might draw our attention away from the central figure. In St John's gospel the emphasis is more on Jesus' victory. The slapping, scourging and mockery had already been administered during the trial. Jesus himself carries his own cross. No record is given of the mockery attendant upon his suffering as he dies. The inscription, King of the Jews, is there, in three languages for all the world to see. Jesus shows loving care for those closest to his affections: a new family is brought together at the foot of the cross. He says, 'I am thirsty', and we are reminded of the reality of his life draining away in a cruel parched death.

St Mark records that terrible cry of desertion, and a little later mentions the death-cry as Jesus breathes his last. John omits 'My God, my God, why . . .?' but includes the last recorded words from the cross, 'It is fulfilled'. All through the fourth gospel, John has included mention of the approach of 'the hour'. Jesus had spoken of the moment when the Son of Man would be lifted up, when he would be glorified, when his task would be complete. Now the hour has come for the completion of that task. 'It is fulfilled.' Against all the evil forces, now unmasked in all their terror, he has completed his Father's task. He, the victor, has overcome.

The two of us plan to meet today, as we have done every Good Friday since we both came to Liverpool. On this occasion we do not raise any of our normal working agenda. We take time to share our own deep thoughts about our Saviour and his Passion. Each year we have felt particularly close as brothers in Christ at that moment when we deliberately meet at the foot of the cross. St John suggests that a new family is coming together at the foot of the cross, when Jesus gives his mother and the beloved disciple to each other. It is a natural ecumenical moment, when Christians of different traditions set aside the differences which have emerged through history and go back to the moment of their redemption, to the very heart of their faith.

St John emphasizes the victory of Christ: it is victory arrived at by the route of suffering, sacrificial love, and perfect obedience to his Father's will. There are times when apparently some Christians want to hurry past Good Friday to Easter and Pentecost. They want to stress the victory of Christ in the Resurrection and the outpouring of the Holy Spirit. Sometimes this can lead them on to portray the Christian journey as healing, security and smiles all the way.

If that were the true and ordinary way to discipleship, it would turn upside down what we see of the Incarnation in the gospels. In fact the Resurrection is a vindication of the way chosen by Jesus, not its reversal. If we are to be his followers, we must expect to use his weapons of love and of respect for people's freedom. The journey will include some of the weakness, struggle and rejection of the suffering Servant. Failure and pain are likely to be part of it. Sometimes we are indeed called to be with Christ in the wilderness, out of which comes good news by the only route which makes it possible for the dispossessed of this world to hear.

Last year, in Holy Week, a West Indian friend wrote explaining some of the hurt he feels that the Church seems so slow in giving black people their full place in its life and mission. He wrote of his recollections of growing up in the Caribbean, where he recalled two types of Christianity: there was the variety which he summed up as 'Servants, obey your masters in the Lord'; and there was the kind represented by the crowded churches on Good Friday, full of people (especially men) who never darkened the church doors at Christmas or Easter, but made a point of being there. The Jesus of the Cross, he wrote, victim of human power, totally identifying himself with people in their suffering, made perfect sense to him. This was his grandmother's religion and his parents' religion.

In a prosperous country like Britain, the dispossessed of the world can easily become invisible. Although, taking account of the whole nation, they are a comparatively small minority, yet in inner cities and perimeter estates, poverty and exclusion from the opportunities of prosperity are the experience of very large numbers of people. In the 'Two-Thirds World' the poor are the great majority. For them the God who chose the way of Golgotha makes perhaps the only sense there is to be made of their deprivation and suffering. Somehow they know that from the cross he understands and reaches out to them.

> *Saviour of the world,*
> *we marvel at the salvation you have accomplished:*
> *help us to walk with you in the way of the cross,*
> *together with your other children,*
> *and to discover your victory*
> *through failure and pain.*
> *We make this prayer*
> *that our Father's name may be glorified. Amen.*

Holy Saturday

(Psalm 41:3, 5; 42:3–4 [42:2, 4; 43:3–4])

My soul is thirsting for God,
the God of my life;
When can I enter and see
the face of God?
Psalm 41:3 [42:2]

Today Christians find themselves at the tomb where the body of their Lord has been reverently placed by family and friends. We think with sorrow and wonder about his passion, death and descent among the dead. With prayer and hopeful faith we await the resurrection.

The terrible aftermath of the events on Golgotha yields only slowly to the mounting expectation that all is not yet over. In churches of the Catholic tradition the altars are stripped bare and in a sense remind us of the tomb itself; for it is there that our Lord's body is to be laid. The altar cloths, like the winding sheets, have been removed. The altar candles are gone, as if to make way for the new light which is to break upon the world, banishing the darkness of sin and death.

New water has been prepared for the empty font. Outside in the vestry spring flowers are gathered in buckets and pails, ready to symbolize the new life which is about to burst forth from the tomb of the world's surface. The Easter garden is ready for the Risen Lord.

But just now it is not only the church buildings which have that feeling of emptiness. Our hearts are riven at what Jesus endured for our sake. It is the same sort of feeling today as often follows a family funeral: that feeling of being somehow without direction, lifted only by thankfulness and hope for the one who has gone before us. In Bach's *St Matthew Passion* the last great chorus surrounds him with 'Lie thou softly, softly lie'. Meanwhile life goes on: it is difficult to keep going, yet we know we must. We are somehow trapped within that cave where the Lord's tomb lies, aching in our emptiness, our minds constantly drifting back to what has happened: the routine of the year shattered once more by the realization of the terrible price paid for our redemption . . .

The wound in Jesus' side is a true sign of the human heart of the Son of God, broken with love for us. The cross itself has become the all-time symbol of salvation; that circlet of thorns a symbol of enduring, unconquerable love.

Even as we think of the emptiness which has gripped our hearts and somehow filled our churches, already the Marys and Marthas of this generation are beginning to move about again, making preparations for tonight's celebration, when the light of Christ will once more show us the way of the Risen Lord, who is truth and life. A latter-day John is beginning to replace some of the furnishings removed from the church for our commemorations of these last days. In the spirit of Joseph of Arimathaea, the parish handyman appears with a ladder to replace the cracked window. Yet in front of the altar, the tomb, we, the companions to whom has been entrusted so much, continue to watch and wait and pray.

Father of our crucified Saviour,
you teach us in both the Old and the New Testament
to celebrate this Passover mystery.
Help us to understand your great love for us.
May the goodness you now show us
confirm our hope in your future mercy.
We ask this through Jesus Christ our Lord. Amen.

Group material

Starting points

Holy Week is a journey in itself, from the triumphal entry of Jesus into Jerusalem on Palm Sunday, through his passion and death to his rising from the dead.

• How did you feel as we moved through the events of Holy Week?
• How does it affect your daily activities?

Deeper reflection

Each day of Holy Week gives rich food for reflection. Groups may wish to choose just one day and spend longer in prayer at this last meeting.

Palm Sunday

• Does the description of Jesus' entry into Jerusalem surprise you?
• When have you ever experienced pressure 'to go along with the crowd'?

Monday: the story of Mary anointing the feet of Jesus

- What does this story say to you?
- What service would you like to have offered Jesus during these days?

Maundy Thursday

- How would you have felt if the Lord had wanted to wash your feet?
- Is it difficult to allow others to 'wash your feet'?
- When have you ever wanted to pray, 'Let this cup pass me by . . .'?

Good Friday

We cannot hurry past Good Friday.

- Take time to stand, in prayer, at the foot of the cross.
- Who also stands there in our world today?

Easter Sunday

- How does Easter Sunday feel?
- When have you ever known new life to come, where there seemed to be only defeat and despair?
- What gives you hope for the future?

Prayer

Retread, in prayer, the journey of Holy Week, using two or three lines chosen from each of the readings in turn and giving time in between them.

- Ask yourselves, in prayer, what has been the gift of this Lenten journey for you? What is the call from this Lent to you?
- Thank God for both.
- Finish with a sign of peace.

Easter Sunday

(John 20:1–9)

It was very early on the first day of the week and still dark, when Mary of Magdala came to the tomb. She saw that the stone had been moved away from the tomb and came running to Simon Peter and the other disciple, the one whom Jesus loved. 'They have taken the Lord out of the tomb,' she said, 'and we don't know where they have put him.'

So Peter set out with the other disciple to go to the tomb. They ran together, but the other disciple, running faster than Peter, reached the tomb first; he bent down and saw the linen cloths lying on the ground, but did not go in. Simon Peter, following him, also came up, went into the tomb, saw the linen cloths lying on the ground and also the cloth that had been over his head; this was not with the linen cloths but rolled up in a place by itself. Then the other disciple who had reached the tomb first also went in; he saw and he believed. Till this moment they had still not understood the scripture, that he must rise from the dead.

John 20:1–9

'Christ is risen, Alleluia!' That is our greeting today. We know what has happened. He has risen, even as he said he would. But for the women going to the tomb to anoint their loved one's body, there is at first inevitable consternation. The body is gone. Later, as we know, the early reports of the body's disappearance give way to graphic accounts of his appearance to his disciples and his friends. Those who merely heard the first reports were incredulous. Once they had seen him they had no doubts. As St Peter was to say later to those who questioned the first miracle he worked in the name of Christ: 'It was you who accused the Holy and Upright One, you who demanded that a murderer should be released to you while you killed the prince of life. God, however, raised him from the dead, and to that fact we are witnesses' (Acts 3:14–15).

Peter was very sure of his facts after the event. At the time described in today's Reading, all was confusion. In advance no one could have imagined what happened. We have the benefit of hindsight. Moreover in this country Christians easily connect Easter with spring. It is natural to speak in the same breath of the new life of daffodils and lambs coming after the frost and death of winter. Of course in countries like Australia, where Easter falls in the autumn, it is the time of leaves withering, dying and falling to the ground. This rather obvious point is perhaps worth making, because tying up Easter so closely with the spring can lead us to think of it as part of the predictable cycle of the seasons.

It is very significant that the resurrection of Jesus Chrst was *not* part of an inevitable process. Try to read today's gospel as if you are hearing it for the first time. Mary Magdalen, Peter and John do not expect Jesus to have risen from the dead: far from it. They were bruised and despairing after the events of Holy Week. They had seen all their most cherished hopes and ideals smashed: truth, goodness, love and gentleness had been crushed by power politics and by the ruthless efficiency of the most powerful military machine in the world. Once you fell into its hands, you did not escape. For the disciples, along with that overwhelming grief went a dreadful memory of their own personal failure and the cold finality of the dead body of Jesus being taken down from the cross.

People sometimes suggest that it is hard to believe in the resurrection 'nowadays'. That word 'nowadays' carries the impression that it was easy to believe at the beginning. But the first disciples knew, just as clearly as any of us, that death is cold and final. The last thing the women expected to find that morning was that the tomb was empty. What they and the disciples saw convinced them that something altogether unpredictable had truly happened – and they were ready to risk their lives for the rest of their days, telling people that the Lord had risen from the dead.

Spring is part of the regular cycle of the seasons. On the other hand, the rising of Jesus Christ from the dead breaks out from the human cycle of birth, growth, decay and death. The resurrection also breaks out from other cycles and patterns which we assume to be unchangeable, like the cycle of good intentions, forces of evil, selfishness, weakness, defeatism, guilt and remorse. It was from the deepest, darkest moment of defeat for all that was true and noble, that the resurrection broke out. 'In fact, Christ has been raised from the dead, as the first-fruits of all who have fallen asleep' (1 Corinthians 15:20).

Those words of St Paul are brought together in the well-loved music of Handel's *Messiah* with the even better-known words, 'I know that my Redeemer liveth'. Isobel Baillie, who sang them so often, said that, when she was preparing herself to sing that aria, 'I know that my Redeemer liveth', she would think of being at the graveside of a loved one. We are both faced with the challenge of those words when we are asked to give the address at a funeral. Sometimes those who are grieving the loss of a partner, or a parent or a child look at us; are they perhaps thinking, 'Never mind the beautiful words. Do you *really* believe now? Can you expect us to do the same?' The united answer is, 'Yes. We do really believe. We believe in the resurrection of the body.' By that we mean not that you will look exactly as you do now, but that all that is best and truest about the person that is you will be taken up, glorified, and made fully alive in the new life of Jesus Christ. 'As it was by one man that death came, so through one man has come the resurrection of the dead. Just as all die in Adam, so in Christ all will be brought to life' (1 Corinthians 15:21–22).

If we are ready to believe that, we shall entertain some great expectations about the world in which we find ourselves now, instead of the defeatist assumptions which seem so often to prevail. Easter Day brings hope here and now with the presence of our risen Lord. His resurrection was the vindication of his way of patient, sacrificial love. His methods continue to be the love which makes the first move, which endures through failures, which does not force itself on others. If we follow him in his way, we shall also meet frustration and suffering; but in his hands those experiences can become the raw materials out of which character and values are fashioned – like faith, hope and love – which last for ever, in spring, summer, autumn, winter, and in his resurrection life which is to come.

Today we are the witnesses at the empty sepulchre. We know what has happened. We rejoice and proclaim: Christ has died; Christ is risen; Christ will come again.

Our mighty God and Father,
you broke the power of the last enemy of the universe
in raising your Son Jesus Christ from the dead.
We pray for all those who today face death,
bereavement, suffering, frustration and hardship.
May they know the presence of the Lord of Life
and step into their future with hope.
We ask this through Jesus Christ our Lord,
who lives and reigns with you and the Holy Spirit,
one God for ever. Amen.

How Many Light-Years to
BABYLON?

Story & Art by
Douman Seiman

CONTENTS

UNNH.
UNNNH.

HANG ON A LITTLE LONGER.

HUFF!

HOW FAR 'TIL THE NEXT PLANET?

HUFF!

WHERE DO YOU WANNA GO?

WE'VE GOT A BUNCH OF PLANETS WITHIN RANGE.

COMPASSIONATE, FALL IN LOVE EASILY.

B.E.M. CREATURES.

PLANET NELSON.

THE PLANET WITH THE BEST GIRLS.

LUNGE

GIRLS.

I'LL SEARCH THE DATABASE.

PUT A PIN IN THAT ONE.

......

USUALLY EAT THEIR MALE PARTNER AFTER INTERCOURSE.

FAIRLY OPEN WHEN IT COMES TO SEX, PARTICULARLY ENJOYS ORAL.

SILICON-BASED LIFE.

PLANET SORITES.

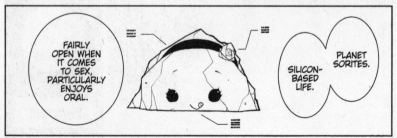

PLANET BERTRAND.

HUMAN-OID.

NOT VERY SMART, BUT VERY STRONG SEXUAL APPETITE.

ONE ROUND OF INTERCOURSE TAKES THIRTY TO FIFTY THOUSAND YEARS.

PIN IT.

THAT'S THE PLACE!!

GO!

Bertrand

5

BAM

THE AVERAGE HEIGHT OF THE WOMEN ON BERTRAND IS SIXTEEN HUNDRED METERS.

. . . . .

IT'S ROUGHLY A **TEN-MINUTE WALK** FROM THE NIPPLES TO THE CLIT.

OOHH?

YOINK
ヒョイ
ヒョイ

HEY!

THAT'S MY SHIP!!

WHAT'S THE BIG IDEA?!

AAH! THIS FEELS SO GOOOOOD.

IT'S BECAUSE YOU LEFT IT IDLING.

MY POOR SHIP!

VRZZ VRZZ VRZZ VRZZ VRZZ

LUCKY!

I FOUND A VIBRATOR!

VRZZ VRZZ VRZZ VRZZ VRZZ VRZZ VRZZ

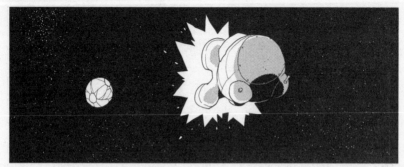

HUFF!

NEXT PLANET!

HURRY.

HUFF!

THE SEATS ARE SOAKED.

THAT WAS A BAD SCENE.

?

SPROING

THIS **PUBE** CAME OUT OF NOWHERE AND TIED ME UP.

WHAT ARE YOU DOING?

AND WHICH GIRL WOULD YOU LIKE?

RIGHT THIS WAY.

THE ONE ON THE TOP RIGHT.

• • • •

VERY GOOD.

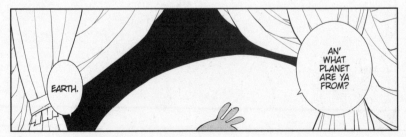

EARTH.

AN' WHAT PLANET ARE YA FROM?

PARDON ME.

AIN'T IT REAL HOMEY?

TRAN-SCENDS SPACE AND TIME, SO I CAN SHOW CLIENTS THE PLACE THEY'RE LOOKIN' FOR.

MY WOMB'S CONNECTED TO A **HIGHER DIMENSION.**

DRINKS ARE ON THE HOUSE, SO GO ON AND HAVE YER FILL.

NYOON

SHK

SHK SHK

SHK

OW OW OW OW OW OW!

SHLK

THIS'LL TAKE A BIT O' ROUGH TREATMENT, THEN.

ZSH ZSH ZSH

ZSH ZSH ZSH

I LOST MY MEMORY, THOUGH.

GOODNESS! YOU DID?!

WANT A CLOSER LOOKIE-LOO?

EARTH?

. . . . .

THAT'S ...

13

14

#3

OH, YOU! SO NAUGHTY!

I WANT YOU TO HAVE MY BABY.

POK

AH!

OOH! RIGHT THERE!

WHMP スコ

WHMP スコ

I FEEL SO EMPTY.

AAAH.

WE CAN'T HAVE ANY OF THAT, SIR.

CRACK

CRACK

KA WHAM

BUT...IT'S NOT LIKE I *DON'T* WANT TO, EITHER.

IT'S NOT LIKE I *WANT* TO HAVE SEX.

YOU MIND GIVING ME A LIFT TO THE NEXT PLANET?

IF YOU'RE A TRAVELER...

YOU'RE NOT FROM THIS PLANET, ARE YOU?

HEY THERE!

I CAN ASK HOPPER.

·····

I'M HITCH-HIKING!

YOU'RE A LIFESAVER!

SURE, TOOTS.

UNNH...

I'M JUNK HEAP.

NAME'S HOPPER.

I'M KARELLEN!

.....

BUB.

WHAT'S YOUR NAME?

IS HE OKAY?

GOING BACK TO THE HOTEL.

I'M...

HE'S A SURVIVOR FROM EARTH.

NOT REALLY.

EARTH? YOU MEAN *THE* EARTH?!

**The Debris Field
Formerly Known as Earth**

GRAB THAT!

OH!

OKAY.

SIGH!

I'D ALWAYS DREAMED OF VISITING EARTH...BUT NOW...

WONDER WHAT THIS IS...

MAYBE A THRONE?

GOT MYSELF A PRECIOUS EARTH RELIC!

I JUST WANT TO PRESERVE EARTH'S LOST CULTURE.

WHAT ARE YOU TALKING ABOUT?

DIGGING THROUGH THE REMNANTS OF A DESTROYED PLANET IS JUST GHOULISH.

LET'S GET GOING.

HM?

WHAT'S THAT THERE?

HE'S TORTURED BY AN ALL-ENCOMPASSING NEED TO PRESERVE HIS SPECIES.

HUNH. SO...

HE'S THE ONLY EARTHLING IN THE WHOLE UNIVERSE.

19

4

JUST DON'T GET THE SEAT WET.

THEY'RE STILL GOING AT IT BACK THERE.

EACH TIME WE DO IT, OUR ODDS OF CONCEIVING GO UP!

HUFF!

BREAK TIME.

IT'S A CLASSIC SHIP. IT CAN'T GO ANY FASTER.

I DO APOLOGIZE FOR THE "LAZINESS."

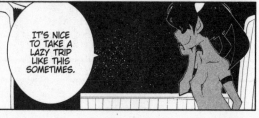

IT'S NICE TO TAKE A LAZY TRIP LIKE THIS SOMETIMES.

I WORK AS A VOLUNTEER TO ENCOURAGE THE PROGRESS OF DEVELOPING PLANETS.

IT'S A GOOD SHIP.

DON'T SULK, HOPPER!

WOW! PRETTY NOBLE.

WHY ARE YOU PLANET HOPPING ANYWAY, KARELLEN?

BUB BASICALLY REMEMBERS NOTHING ABOUT IT.

I EVEN WENT TO EARTH ONCE, Y'KNOW.

TELL ME ABOUT EARTH!!

YOU DID?!

IT JUST DOESN'T CLICK WHEN PEOPLE CALL ME THAT...

I'M PRETTY SURE MY NAME'S NOT ACTUALLY BUB.

EVEN HIS NAME'S A MYSTERY. "BUB" WAS JUST SOMETHING PRINTED ON HIS CLOTHES WHEN WE FOUND HIM.

I GUESS HIS NAME IS BUB?

YEP, IT SAYS "SPONGE BUB" IN ONE OF THE EARTH LANGUAGES.

I SHARED SOME OF OUR TECHNOLOGY WITH THIS BEARDED GUY WHO WAS PASSING BY.

EARTH BEINGS WERE STILL QUITE PRIMITIVE BACK THEN.

SORRY, BUT IT'S BEEN A LONG TIME SINCE I WENT TO EARTH.

SORRY IT'S NOT MORE HELPFUL.

THAT'S MY MEMORY OF EARTH.

LIKE THIS GRAVITATIONAL CONTROL UNIT SO STRONG YOU COULD WALK ON WATER.

AND A MOLECULAR CONVERTER TO TURN WATER INTO WINE.

BUT HIS DISCIPLES THREW ROCKS AT ME, SO I TOOK OFF.

YOU MIGHT LEARN SOMETHING ABOUT EARTH!

THAT'S WHERE THE RECORDS OF THE UNIVERSE ARE, RIGHT?

OH?

I WANT TO KNOW...

WHY WAS I THE ONLY ONE TO SURVIVE?

WHY THE EARTH WAS DESTROYED.

WE'RE HEADING FOR AKASHA NEXT.

24

IF I'M PREGNANT, I'LL MAKE SURE TO RAISE THE KID RIGHT.

THANKS.

I HOPE YOU HAVE A SAFE TRIP.

THANKS FOR THE RIDE!

I HOPE WE CAN MEET UP AGAIN SOMETIME.

BYE!

WE'RE BACK TO AN ALL-MALE HOUSEHOLD.

YUP.

QUIT YAPPING.

YOU'LL RUIN THE MOMENT.

A TOTAL SHITHEAD, BUT--

I'M, WELL...

26

#5

OH!

KAITEN SUSHI!

YOU WANT TO STOP?

I'M STARVING.

YEAH.

THERE WAS PROBABLY SOMETHING LIKE IT ON EARTH.

IT'S THIS DISH WHERE THEY PUT SEAFOOD ON TOP OF A GRAIN.

WHAT'S KAITEN SUSHI?

TABLE.

TABLE SEAT OR COUNTER SEAT?

WELCOME TO BIG CRUNCH SUSHI!

HOW FAR DOES THIS BELT GO?

WOW.

TAKE WHAT YOU WANT FROM THE BELT.

PAR... SEX?

A TOTAL OF 0.003 PARSECS.

THIS BELT'S THE LONGEST IN THE UNIVERSE!

THAT MEANS NOTHING TO ME.

ABOUT NINE TERAMETERS.

THE CHEF'S MAKING SUSHI, RIGHT?

TAKE A LOOK OVER THERE.

SEE?

THE BELT'S MOVING AT 4.8 METERS A MINUTE.

HE SETS IT ON THE BELT.

TAK

IT'S LIKE FLICKERING STARLIGHT. ROMANTIC, HUH?

I'M GETTING DIZZY.

IT'LL TAKE 1.19 MILLION YEARS FOR THAT PLATE TO GET HERE.

IT'S THREE TERAMETERS FROM THERE TO THIS TABLE.

IS THIS ACTUALLY EDIBLE?

THESE PLATES WERE MADE 1.19 MILLION YEARS AGO.

IN OTHER WORDS...

30

AND IS BROUGHT RIGHT TO OUR MOUTHS.

EACH PLATE TRAVERSES THIS GREAT UNIVERSE...

THERE'S ABSOLUTELY NO REASON TO MAKE IT GO AROUND.

THAT'S A GOOD POINT.

YOU JUST DON'T GET IT, JUNK.

HOPPER, SOMETIMES I CAN'T TELL IF YOU'RE A ROMANTIC... OR JUST DISTURBED.

THIS SUSHI'S A **TRAVELER**, JUST LIKE US.

ACTUALLY, AN EARTHLING'S DELICATE MOUTH CAN'T HANDLE THIS, EITHER.

NOW I EAT!

OKAY! HERE YA GO!

EARTHLINGS ARE A PAIN IN THE ASS.

SO THIS IS SUSHI...

32

6

I-IT WASN'T MY FAULT...!

GOD-DAMN IT!

YOU SCRATCHED IT, JUNK!

AAH!

IT'S THAT SHIP'S FAULT.

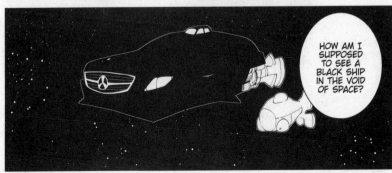

HOW AM I SUPPOSED TO SEE A BLACK SHIP IN THE VOID OF SPACE?

VWEEN

LOOKS LIKE WE NEED TO SORT THIS OUT.

GAH!

DO-GOHKAN!

NOW YOU'VE DONE IT.

AAAH.

MIND ACCOMPANYING US TO OUR OFFICE?

CRAP...

Dogohk 893

I TRUST YOU'LL PAY FOR THE REPAIRS?

SO, BOYS...

YOU TWO WILL WORK IN THE GALTITE MINES.

THEN HOW ABOUT YOU PAY WITH YOUR FLESH?

WE CAN'T AFFORD THAT!

FIVE MILLION SPACE YEN?

35

I'VE BOUGHT BEFORE, BUT I'VE NEVER BEEN SOLD.

THAT ESCALATED QUICKLY.

EEP!

YOU, THOUGH. YOU'VE GOT NICE SKIN. YOU'LL WORK AT OUR SHOP.

AH.

YOU HAVE A GREAT BODY.

OH! NEW GUY?

AAH! IT'S MY FIRST TIME! MY FIRST TIME!!

YOU'RE PRETTY CUTE YOURSELF!

36

YOUSE CAN GO.

REALLY?

WE EARNED FIVE MILLION ALREADY?!

HE SAID OUR DEBT'S PAID UP, SO WE CAN GO.

THEY'RE *SUPER* INTO YOU.

WE'LL BE WAITIN' FOR YA.

SQUEEZE

COME BACK ANYTIME!

SQUEEZE

SKREEE

38

7

SO, I WAS THINKING ABOUT THIS BACK ON DOGOHK.

IT DOESN'T MAKE SENSE TO TOSS IT ALL OVER THE UNIVERSE, THOUGH.

YOU'VE SPREAD YOUR SEED ON EVERY PLANET WE'VE BEEN TO.

YOU DON'T *HAVE* TO BE A MAN ANYMORE, BUB.

BUT I CAN'T TURN INTO A WOMAN.

THAT *IS* TRUE.

IF YOU WERE A WOMAN, YOU COULD GET PREGNANT AND HAVE THE KID WITH YOU.

WHAT DO YOU MEAN?

GENDER REASSIGNMENT IS A PRETTY EASY PROCEDURE IN SPACE.

SURE YOU CAN!

HE MIGHT NOT LOOK LIKE IT, BUT JUNK'S A DOCTOR.

40

41

42

AND HERE WE GO AGAIN WITH YOUR EARTHLING HANG-UPS.

THAT'S JUST STRAIGHT-UP WRONG!

NO! NO WAY!

I CAN'T DO *THAT!*

EVEN IF THE PLANET'S OKAY WITH IT, I'M NOT!

IT'S NOT AGAINST THE LAW ON THIS PLANET. YOU'RE FINE.

AND YET, IT ALSO **SOLVES** NOTHING.

HUNH. WELL, PROBLEM SOLVED.

HEY, GIRL-FRIEND!

WANNA HAVE SOME FUN?

44

8

MMM?

NNN...

WELL, WE'LL KEEP AN EYE ON YOU FOR THE TIME BEING.

LOOKS LIKE THE NANO-MACHINES DIDN'T TAKE PROPERLY.

HUH? MY BODY'S BACK TO NORMAL.

HM?

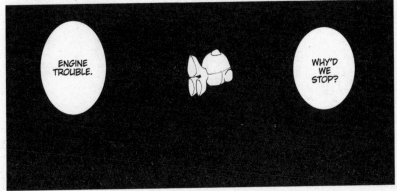

ENGINE TROUBLE.

WHY'D WE STOP?

THIS IS **THE VOID,** A SPACE OUTSIDE ANY GALAXY.

THERE AREN'T ANY STARS OR LIFE-FORMS HERE.

HOPPER'S GONE TO TAKE A LOOK.

CAN'T CALL A TOW TRUCK, EITHER.

NOT A SINGLE STAR AROUND, HUH?

AND HOPPER'S AN **ABSOLUTE BEING.** HE CAN LIVE A THOUSAND YEARS IN SPACE WITHOUT EATING OR DRINKING.

I'M FINE SO LONG AS I GOT A BIT OF OIL.

WHY JUST ME?!

WORST CASE, YOU MIGHT STARVE TO DEATH.

46

OH!

THERE YOU ARE.

REALLY? *HOPPER?* I HAD NO IDEA.

I'M GONNA GO SEE HOW HE'S DOING.

I GUESS THE NANO-MACHINE THINGS DIDN'T TAKE.

AND YOU'RE BACK TO YOUR OLD BODY.

I CAN'T FIT INSIDE THE DAMAGED AREA.

IT'S NO USE.

WELL, WE'RE SCREWED IF YOU CAN'T.

47

48

BETTER GET SOME REPAIRS DONE WHILE YOUR BODY'S STILL HANGING ON!

WOW!

THE NANO-MACHINES WILL PICK UP THE SLACK.

IT'S OKAY!

GOD!

I KNEW THIS WAS A BAD IDEA!!

BUT YOUR BODY'S STARTING TO DIE, SINCE IT'S NOT GETTING ANY SIGNALS FROM THE BRAIN.

TWITCH TWITCH

WOULD I EVEN BE **HUMAN** ANYMORE?

IF MY BODY DIES, WILL I BE STUCK LIKE THIS MY WHOLE LIFE?

HM.

KA CHAK

GUESS IT GOT KNOCKED LOOSE.

IS THIS THE POWER SOURCE?

HE FIXED IT?

VRR VRR

VRR VRR

OH!

EH, IT WAS CLOSE.

YOU SAVED ME.

Phew!

I TAKE IT ALL BACK!

ALMOST PUT YOUR HEAD ON BACKWARDS THERE.

YER CUTTING IT CLOSE!

HOW'S MY BODY?!

HYOO

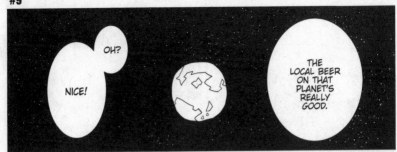

9

I CAN'T DRIVE LIKE THIS.

YOU SURE?

DON'T SCRATCH IT.

HEY, LEMME DRIVE!

YOU SURE?

THE CLUTCH.

WHAT'S THIS OTHER ONE?

ACCELERATOR. BRAKE.

FWOOSH

KAWHUNK

NO LICENSE AND DRIVING UNDER THE INFLUENCE.

IT'S THE SPACE PATROL!

IT'S PRISON FOR YOU, BUDDY.

THAT'S THE PRISON PLANET.

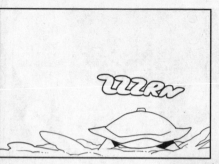

THIS'LL BE A PIECE OF CAKE.

ZZZRN

WHAT? JUST THREE HOURS?

WE'LL COME BACK FOR YOU IN THREE HOURS.

I CAN'T MOVE!

THIS GRAVITY...

TH--

PWAP

IT'S JUST FOR THREE HOURS.

STAGGER

BUT...

I GUESS THE PLANET'S ROTATING REALLY FAST?

THE STARS ARE SHOOTING THROUGH THE SKY.

FWUMP

PWAP

KRR KRR KRR

THEY'RE BACK!

!

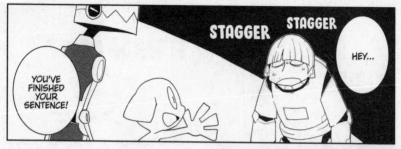

56

10

THIS IS AKASHA.

WE FINALLY MADE IT.

IS A FACILITY TO STORE THE HISTORY OF THE ENTIRE UNIVERSE SINCE ITS CREATION.

THE WHOLE PLANET...

WOW.

NIGHT PACK, PLEASE.

I HAVE A MEMBER'S CARD.

WELCOME.

IS THIS YOUR FIRST VISIT TO OUR LIBRARY?

YOU CAN HAVE AS MUCH ICE CREAM AS YOU WANT, TOO!

YOU'VE BEEN HERE BEFORE, HOPPER?

MAKE YOUR-SELVES AT HOME.

PLEASE, HELP YOURSELVES TO DRINKS AT THE CORNER IN THE BACK.

HUH?! SO WE **DIDN'T** HAVE TO COME ALL THE WAY TO THE CENTER OF THE UNIVERSE?!

IT'S MY FIRST TIME AT THIS ONE.

BUT THEY HAVE 480,000 BRANCHES ACROSS THE UNIVERSE.

FLIP

PLUS, I'VE ALWAYS WANTED TO COME HERE.

THE MAIN BRANCH HAS THE LARGEST SELECTION.

THEY'LL **FOR SURE** HAVE RECORDS OF EARTH!

SO, THESE ARE THE RECORDS OF THE UNIVERSE, HUH?

SHFF

BY AS MANY BEINGS IN THE UNIVERSE AS POSSIBLE.

THE PICTORIAL FORMAT WAS ADOPTED SO THE INFORMATION COULD BE UNDERSTOOD ...

MANGA?!

IT'S GONNA BE HARD TO FIND ANYTHING HERE.

BUT...

I WILL.

WE'RE HEADING TO OUR ROOM.

YOU GO LOOK FOR RECORDS OF EARTH.

OH! FRONT DESK LADY!

CAN I HELP YOU?

THERE'S A SHUTTLE BUS.

I'LL SHOW YOU THE WAY.

AT THE START OF BLOCK SIX.

EARTH... EARTH IS...

PLEASE LET ME KNOW IF I CAN BE OF ASSISTANCE.

I'M THE LIBRARIAN, **AKASHIYA**.

I'M LOOKING FOR RECORDS OF EARTH.

62

THIS IS THE SECTION ON EARTH.

WE'VE ARRIVED.

TOUGH JOB.

PSSSHT

I CAN'T READ ALL THAT!

THERE'S A TOTAL OF SIX HUNDRED THIRTY MILLION VOLUMES.

THE HISTORY OF EARTH IS COMPLETE.

YEAH.

MAYBE THIS'LL JOG YOUR MEMORY!

OH, HEY! YOU'RE BACK.

BORROWED THE LAST FEW VOLUMES.

I JUST...

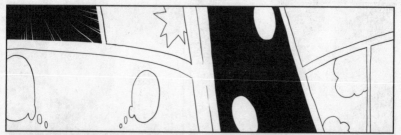

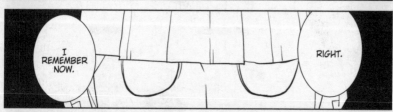

I REMEMBER NOW.

RIGHT.

I...

11

I'VE ALWAYS DREAMED OF COMING TO JAPAN!

WOW! SO THIS IS AKIHABARA!

I'M FINALLY HERE!

Sign: Electron

Right sign: Ondeno
Left sign: World Radio Building

I'VE ALWAYS WANTED TO TRY IT!

SO, THIS IS KAITEN SUSHI!

LOOK AT ALL THESE FIGURES AND MANGA! THEY DON'T SELL ANY OF THIS STUFF IN ENGLAND!

HOLY CRAP!

I'LL GO TO IKEBUKURO NEXT.

TACHI-KAWA'S FAR.

THEN NOBORITO.

ENTRANCE

NOW, WHERE SHALL I GO TOMORROW?

WOW, THAT WAS A BLAST!

SPONGE '09 BOBS

MY WALLET'S GONE!

IT'S GONE!

HM?

HUH?

DIG

66

ALONE IN A FOREIGN COUNTRY... I DON'T THINK I'VE EVER FELT SO HELPLESS.

BLOODY HELL. WHAT AM I GONNA DO?

YOU IN TROUBLE?

HEY, WHAT'S WRONG?

ATM

I WENT THERE ON MY GRADUATION TRIP.

EN-GLAND?

LONDON, MANCHESTER, LIVERPOOL.

IT'S A NICE COUNTRY.

OKAY.

SOMEONE MIGHT FIND IT.

WELL, LET'S GO FILE A REPORT WITH THE POLICE.

OH, WOW.

MINEHEAD. IT'S IN ENGLAND.

WHERE ARE YOU FROM?

· · · · ·

WHERE ARE YOU STAYING TONIGHT?

KOBAN

TRAFFIC SAFETY

PEOPLE 0

THANK YOU VERY MUCH.

THAT'S TOO MUCH!

I CAN'T LET YOU DO THAT. I JUST MET YOU!

NO!

I COULD LEND YOU HOTEL MONEY?

SHAKE

SHAKE

YOU DON'T LOOK LIKE YOU ARE.

I'M PRETTY USED TO SLEEPING ROUGH.

DON'T WORRY ABOUT ME. I'LL CAMP OUT AROUND HERE.

C'MON!

I KNOW!

AND YOU CAN THINK ABOUT LATER... LATER.

WE'LL JUST DRINK 'TIL MORNING!

LET'S GO GRAB A DRINK.

IF YOU WON'T LET ME PAY FOR YOUR HOTEL, AT LEAST LET ME TREAT YOU TO A DRINK.

THANKS.

OKAY.

YOU'VE BEEN ASLEEP FOR **TWO** DAYS.

YOU READ THAT BOOK AND COLLAPSED.

WHOA. YOU AWAKE?

......

69

BUT I DO KNOW ONE THING.

I STILL CAN'T RECALL WHY THE EARTH WAS DESTROYED.

NOT THE KEY PART.

MAYBE IT'S BECAUSE MY MEMORY CAME BACK SO SUDDENLY.

YOU GOT YOUR MEMORY BACK, BUB?!

MY NAME'S NOT BUB!

BUB IS THE NAME OF THE CARTOON CHARACTER ON MY T-SHIRT!

MY NAME IS DANIEL!

IT'S SUPER EMBARRASS-ING THAT EVERYONE'S BEEN CALLING ME BY THAT STUPID NAME!

NOW THAT MY MEMORY'S BACK...

BUT WE'RE PRETTY USED TO BUB.

OKAY, THAT'S GREAT...

......

12

BABYLON.

WE DON'T HAVE ANYWHERE LINED UP TO GO.

WELL? WHAT NOW?

HUH?

I GET THIS FEELING THAT I HAVE TO GO TO A PLACE CALLED BABYLON.

I DON'T KNOW WHERE IT IS, THOUGH.

OUR ONLY OPTION IS TO ASK THE FOURTH-DIMENSION MAN.

I GUESS...

SEEMS LIKE YOUR MEMORY'S STILL A LITTLE HAZY.

HMM. EVEN THOUGH YOU JUST REMEMBERED A BUNCH OF STUFF...

HE'S THE MOST RESPECTED BEING IN THE ENTIRE UNIVERSE.

THE 4D MAN IS A GREAT PERSON.

EXCUSE ME?

IS THIS SOME KIND OF A SCAM?

FOURTH DIMENSION?!

HE MIGHT BE THE CLOSEST THING TO IT.

SOUNDS LIKE A GOD.

HE CAN TRAVERSE ALL OF SPACE-TIME, FROM THE BEGINNING OF THE UNIVERSE TO THE END.

HE'S THE ONLY BEING WHO CAN GO BEYOND TIME.

WE'RE ABLE TO CRUISE AROUND SPACE LIKE THIS.

THANKS TO THE FOURTH-DIMENSION MAN...

AN EXPLORER WAS ON AN ADVENTURE TO THE FARTHEST REACHES OF THE UNIVERSE.

ABOUT FIVE BILLION YEARS AGO...

THE 4D MAN SAID..

LONG JOURNEYS MUST BE HARD WITH THAT EQUIPMENT.

HOW ABOUT I LEND YOU MY TOOLS?

AND BECAME THE FIRST PERSON TO MAKE CONTACT WITH THE MAN FROM THE FOURTH DIMENSION.

HE STOPPED AT A DESERTED PLANET ALONG THE WAY...

A SUB-LIGHT-SPEED RADIAL ENGINE...

AND A CHART OF ALL THE WORM-HOLES IN THE UNIVERSE.

A PERPETUAL MOTION BATTERY...

WHAT HE HANDED OVER WERE...

HUNH.

AND SPACE TRAVEL SPREAD EXPLOSIVELY!

THE EXPLORER ACHIEVED THE GREAT FEAT OF MASTERING THE UNIVERSE ...

WITH THOSE TOOLS...

HOW'RE WE GOING TO FIND HIM?

BUT NO ONE KNOWS WHERE THAT GUY IS.

IN FACT, WE COULD ASK HIM TO LOOK AT THE PLANET'S FINAL DAYS.

I'M SURE THE 4D MAN KNOWS ALL ABOUT EARTH, TOO.

MAKES SENSE.

I'VE GOT A GREAT IDEA!

KNOWN FOR THE MOVIE *TREMORS*!

HE'S ONE OF EARTH'S BIG ACTORS!

ON EARTH, THERE'S THIS GAME ABOUT KEVIN BACON.

KEVIN BACON?

74

I CAN ASK THE PERSON CLOSEST TO ME WHO SEEMS MOST LIKELY TO KNOW HIM.

No.

Do you know Bacon?

SO...

IF I WANT TO MEET KEVIN BACON...

WHOA-AA!

REPEAT THAT PATTERN...

AND BY THE SIXTH PERSON, YOU'LL DEFINITELY REACH BACON!

No.

IF THEY DON'T KNOW KEVIN BACON...

Do you know?

THE UNIVERSE IS HUGE, THOUGH, SO WE'LL PROBABLY NEED MORE THAN SIX PEOPLE.

THEY ASK A PERSON NEAR THEM WHO SEEMS LIKE THEY MIGHT.

THIS BACON GUY'S AMAZING.

BUT WE'LL FOR SURE BE ABLE TO GET CLOSER TO THE 4D MAN LIKE THIS!

I'VE GOT JUST THE PLACE.

ANYWAY, WE HAVE TO START SOME-WHERE.

COME ON OVER!

GET 'EM WHILE THEY'RE HOT!

THEY'VE GOT THE LARGEST FOURTH-DIMENSION MAN MUSEUM IN THE UNIVERSE.

THE PLANET SMITHANISON.

IT DOESN'T *FEEL* LIKE HE'S THE MOST RESPECTED BEING IN THE UNIVERSE.

THE FOUNDER'S 4D FRY IS DELICIOUS.

HOW ABOUT 4D MAGNETS AS A SOUVENIR?

WE GOT 4D T-SHIRTS BACK IN STOCK.

13

BAM

THAT COULD BE LOTS OF PEOPLE, DEPENDING ON THE HAND.

THEIR GENDER IS UNKNOWN, AND IT'S SAID YOU CAN COUNT ON ONE HAND THE NUMBER OF PEOPLE WHO HAVE SEEN WHAT LIES BENEATH THE ROBES.

THIS IS THE MOST WIDELY KNOWN FORM OF THE FOURTH-DIMENSION MAN.

NEXT, WE'LL TAKE A LOOK AT THE 4D MAN'S PERSONAL LIFE.

TRUDGE

TRUDGE

THIS TOOTHBRUSH IS SAID TO HAVE BEEN USED BY THE 4D MAN.

NO WAY!

KARELLEN ?!

HOW LONG HAS IT BEEN?!

I'VE BEEN LOOKING FOR YOU FOREVER!

FOR ME?

YOU'VE CHANGED A LOT.

AKKA.

VITA.

COME HERE.

WELL, STUFF HAPPENED.

79

SERI-
OUSLY?!

THESE
ARE OUR
KIDS.

GLANCE

EH...?

NO
WAY.

THEY'RE
ALREADY
SO BIG.

STILL!

THE
PROBABILITY
WASN'T
ZERO!

I
TOLD
YOU,
DIDN'T
I?

80

AKKA, VITA.

I'M YOUR DADDY...

OH, RIGHT!

YOU WERE IN PRISON FOR TEN YEARS.

DID YOU FORGET?

OH! IT'S NOTHING!

WHAT?

SHFF

OH DEAR!

WHEN A STRANGE WOMAN RANDOMLY CLAIMS SHE'S YOUR DADDY, I MEAN...

CAN'T BLAME THEM FOR BEING SKEPTICAL.

DAMMIT! WHY DID I HAVE TO LOOK LIKE THIS TODAY OF ALL DAYS?!

THE POOR MITES NEED A MINUTE TO WRAP THEIR HEADS AROUND IT.

WELL, IT *IS* WEIRD, ME SHOWING UP OUT OF THE BLUE.

THIS IS YOUR EARTHLING DADDY!

I'M ALWAYS TELLING YOU ABOUT HIM, AREN'T I?

MAYBE WE DON'T NEED TO FIND THE 4D MAN NOW?

SO THEN...

THE FIRST STEP TO EARTH'S RECOVERY.

WHAT?

I ACTUALLY KNOW HIM.

HUH?

WHAT?!

KEVIN BACON!!

YEAH.

YOU'RE LOOKING FOR THE 4D MAN?

14

I TOLD YOU I WAS A VOLUNTEER, RIGHT?

BUT I COULD TRY CONTACTING HIM.

I'VE ONLY MET HIM A COUPLE TIMES.

WOW!

THE FOURTH-DIMENSION MAN FUNDS MY WORK.

PLEASE!

SIP SIP

THIS?

HM?

I CAN'T BELIEVE YOU CAN DRINK THAT.

WHEN THEY FALL TO THE GROUND, THEY'RE EATEN BY AN INDIGENOUS CREATURE CALLED THE JEKORANEN.

THE CAFFEINE BEANS GROW ON A TROPICAL PLANET.

IT'S GOOD. IT'S LIKE EARTH COFFEE.

YOU'LL BE SURPRISED WHEN YOU HEAR HOW IT'S MADE.

THE GAPPLY'S EATEN BY A MESEH-BASARA.

THE MESUNCHIRA IS EATEN BY A GAPPLY.

THIS JEKORANEN IS EATEN BY A MESLIN-CHIRA.

THERE WAS A DRINK LIKE THAT ON EARTH, TOO.

SIP SIP

SHOCKING, ISN'T IT?

AND THE UNDIGESTED BEANS THAT COME OUT IN THE MESEHBASARA'S POOP ARE COLLECTED AND ROASTED TO MAKE *THAT*.

84

WHAT A MESS.

I CAN'T BELIEVE IT!

WHAT IS UP WITH EARTHLINGS?!

MOMMY, ME TOO!

AAH, LOOK AT YOU.

THEY'VE GOT A DEVELOPMENTAL DISORDER.

THEY DO?

THE TRUTH IS, THE KIDS?

IT'S NOT THAT THEY DON'T LIKE YOU.

THEY BASICALLY CAN'T COMMUNICATE WITH ANYONE OTHER THAN ME.

KA-SNAP

I'M GOING TO TRY AND BE A GOOD PARENT, TOO.

THANKS FOR BEING SUCH A GREAT MOM.

......

SQUEEZE

I WANT TO BE ABLE TO AT LEAST *TALK* WITH THEM!

AT ANY RATE...

NO! NO, THIS CAN'T BE HAPPENING!

AAH...! YOU'RE--

KAR-ELLEN?!

. . . .

TAKE THE CHILDREN.

CRUMBLE

I WILL!

AH!

PLEASE...

15

I MEAN, THEIR MOM JUST GOT VAPORIZED RIGHT IN FRONT OF THEM!

WELL, OF COURSE.

THE MOOD'S PRETTY HEAVY.

THE KIDS AREN'T SAYING A WORD, EITHER.

THE ZOO!!

WE HAVE TO DECIDE ON OUR NEXT STOP PRETTY QUICK HERE.

SO? WHAT'LL WE DO?

PLEASE! TAKE US TO A ZOO!

IF YOU WANNA MAKE A KID HAPPY, IT'S GOTTA BE THE ZOO!

IT'S THE ZOO!

SEE?

OKAY!

I'M ON IT!

KA-CHAK

The planet Nowayzoo

THIS WAS THE ONLY PLANET NEARBY WHERE YOU CAN LOOK AT ANIMALS.

SORRY.

IT'S NOT *QUITE A* ZOO.

90

SHIELD

DON'T LOOK!

AND ENCOURAGE THEM TO BREED.

THEY ROUND UP ALL THE CREATURES IN THE UNIVERSE IN DANGER OF EXTINCTION...

GAAAAH!

WE KNOW ABOUT COPULATION.

IT'S FINE.

．．．．．

YOUR SEX DRIVE'S GONE, RIGHT?

YEAH. TOTALLY.

．．．．．

CHILDREN ARE SO MATURE THESE DAYS.

THAT REMINDS ME.

NOW I GET ANXIOUS WHEN I LOOK AT THOSE KIDS.

BUT...

92

. . . . .

DON'T CALL ME BUB ANY- MORE.

MY NAME'S DANIEL.

WHAT'S WRONG?

I JUST REALIZED...

MY NAME, SHE...

WITHOUT EVEN KNOWING ...

I NEVER TOLD KARELLEN MY **REAL** NAME.

WAA- AAAH!

WAAA- AAH!

WAA- AAAH!

UNH!

WHERE ARE THE KIDS?

WE SET UP A BED FOR THEM IN THE ENGINE ROOM.

MY DIGNITY AS A FATHER IS GONE.

THAT WAS PATHETIC. AND WITH THE KIDS WATCHING.

MEH, YOU HAD NONE TO START WITH.

BUT HE DOESN'T SEEM LIKE A BAD PERSON.

YEAH.

AKKA?

WHAT?

THAT WAS PATHE-TIC.

WHAT DO YOU THINK OF HIM?

94

16

BEEP BEEP

WHAT WERE YOU THINKING, YOU IDIOT?!

AHH, CRAP.

I GOT TOO CLOSE TO A COMPULSORY TOURISM PLANET.

THEY MADE A RULE THAT YOU HAVE TO LAND AND DO SOME SIGHT-SEEING...

A PLANET FLAGGED BY THE UNIVERSAL TOURISM AS-SOCIATION.

COMPUL-SORY TOURISM PLANET?

ACK! WHAT'S THAT?!

IF YOU APPROACH CERTAIN PLANETS THAT RARELY GET TOURISTS.

AND THE TYKES MIGHT LIKE IT.

JUST A BIT OF A STOP-OVER.

WELL, IT'S NO BIG DEAL.

WHAT A PAIN IN THE ASS.

CRAP!

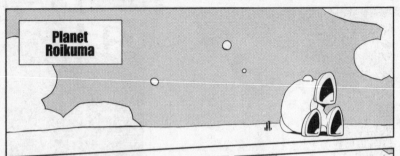

Planet Roikuma

THERE'S NOTHING HERE.

ARE THERE EVEN ANY SIGHTS TO SEE?

OH, THERE ARE!

HMM?

LOOK REAL CLOSE AT THE GROUND.

YAAH!

YAAH!

YAAH!

YOU'VE CRUSHED ABOUT **SIX THOUSAND** OF THEM SO FAR.

INCIDENTALLY...

THE ROIKU-MANS...

GAH!

ARE ABOUT THREE-HUNDREDTHS OUR SIZE.

98

SO?

HOW DO WE GET OFF THIS SHITTY PLANET?

STAMP QUEST, I GUESS.

EEEEK!

FOR THEIR BELOVED TOURISTS...

THEY DON'T MIND DEATH.

YOU WAIT HERE.

DO NOT GET OUT OF THE SHIP.

LET'S HURRY.

MY NANO-MACHINES TO DO THE DETAIL WORK.

I'LL GET...

FILL UP THE STAMP CARD AND SIGHTSEEING'S DONE.

HOW ARE WE SUPPOSED TO STAMP THIS?!

DASH

TO THE FIRST POINT!

HUFF!

HUFF!

NOOOOO!

RIGHT ABOUT NOW, TENS OF THOUSANDS OF ROIKU-MANS...

ARE DIVING INTO YOUR STOMACH.

MY STOMACH'S FULL.

WEIRD.

HUFF!

· · · · ·

URP!

PART OF THEIR HOSPITALITY IS MAKING YOU EAT UNTIL YOU BARF.

AH, YES. THE LOCAL DELICACY...

RAW ROIKUMANS.

THE ROIKU-MANS ARE PRETTY HIGH IN CALORIES.

IT SEEMS...

YOU'VE PUT ON SOME POUNDS.

THIS IS THE FIRST CHECK-POINT.

LET'S GET TO THE NEXT ONE.

AH!

I CAN HANDLE IT.

TELL ME.

NO, NOTHING.

WHAT?

101

17

I'LL COME WITH.

I'LL GO TAKE A LOOK, SEE IF WE CAN'T REPAIR IT.

BUT THEY SAID IT'LL TAKE A WHILE.

I CALLED ROADSIDE ASSISTANCE.

SO WE'RE STUCK HERE?

LEAP

LOOK AT ME! I'M SPACE-WALKING, TOO!

YEAH.

SO COOL...

SO THESE ARE SPACE CLOTHES?

ERK!

PUT YOUR HOOD UP.

FLAIL

FLAIL

YOU DUMMY.

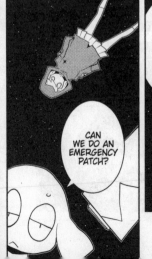

CAN WE DO AN EMERGENCY PATCH?

WE CAN'T REPAIR THIS WITH THE TOOLS WE'VE GOT.

THAT SPACE ROCK MADE A PRETTY BIG HOLE.

AND...

I'M OUT HERE SPACE-WALKING.

BUT THERE'S NOT ACTUALLY THAT MUCH TO DO.

YOU'RE **SCREWED** WITHOUT A TETHER.

OUT HERE...

THERE'S ALREADY NOTHING AROUND ME.

I AM DEFINITELY FLOATING AWAY RIGHT NOW.

HOPPER!

DOES THIS THING HAVE A RADIO?

JUNK!

GOD-DAMMIT! I'M NOT GETTING ANY-WHERE!

FLAIL

ACK! SHIT!

FLAIL

HELP!

SOMEONE!

I HAVE TO PEE.

OH NO.

• • • • •

SPSH

PLSH

PLSH

PLSH

NOPE! THIS IS REGULAR PANTS-PISSING!

DON'T THEY ABSORB PEE AND RECYCLE IT INTO DRINKING WATER?

THESE ARE SPACE CLOTHES, THOUGH.

KOFF! HACK!

AND IT'S HEADING DIRECTLY FOR MY HELMET!!

JUST GONNA TURN INTO A SPECK IN THE UNIVERSE.

I'LL BE THAT GUY WHO DROWNED IN HIS OWN PISS.

I'M GOING TO DIE.

GASP!

CAN'T HAVE THAT!

SO I CAN'T LET YOU DIE SUCH AN EMBARRASSING DEATH.

I KEPT YOU ALIVE BECAUSE I HAVE A PURPOSE FOR YOU YET.

YOU'RE MY SUCCESSOR.

I'M SCARED! SPACE IS SCARY!!

WH-WHAT?!

WHOA.

HE PISSED HIS PANTS.

NOT ON THE SEAT!

UGH!

WHAT'S WRONG, BUB?

EH?

WHAT HAPPENED?

CLOSE CALL! IT ALMOST HIT US.

AH! AN ASTEROID!

HYOOO

PHEW!

108

18

THE ADDRESS ON KARELLEN'S BUSINESS CARD IS AROUND HERE SOMEWHERE.

THIS IS IT.

THIS IS THE VOLUNTEER AGENCY OFFICE, RIGHT?

CAN I HELP YOU?

EXCUSE ME...?

POOR KARELLEN.

I SEE...

I THOUGHT I MIGHT BE ABLE TO MEET THE FOURTH-DIMENSION MAN.

SO, UM...

AND SHE DID SUCH EXCELLENT WORK.

SHE WAS SO DILIGENT.

NEVER, HUH?

SLUMP

BUT THE FOURTH-DIMENSION MAN HAS NEVER SHOWN HIS FACE IN THIS OFFICE.

OH, I'M SORRY. I KNOW YOU'VE COME ALL THE WAY OUT HERE.

YOU CAN TELL JUST LOOKING AT 'EM--THEIR CULTURAL LEVEL'S LOW.

OH, I GET IT.

UMM.

WHAT ARE WE SUPPOSED TO DO?

I SENSE A COERCIVE PREJUDICE IN THAT.

I GUESS PROTRUDING NOSE HAIR ALWAYS EQUALS LOW CULTURAL LEVEL.

FIRST, TIDY UP THEIR NOSE HAIRS.

NO CHARGE!

AND YOU LOW-CULTURE TYPES JUST LOVE ANYTHING FREE, RIGHT?

TO PLUCK YOUR NOSE HAIRS?

WOULD YOU ALLOW ME...

APPARENTLY, BARE FEET IS WITHOUT A DOUBT THE SIGN OF LOW CULTURE.

NEXT IS SHOES.

HEY, C'MERE A SEC.

THOSE LOOK GREAT ON YOU.

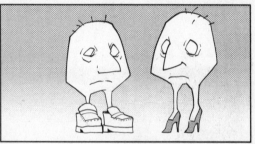

THEIR IMMUNE SYSTEMS GOT WEAKER BECAUSE WE PLUCKED THEIR NOSE HAIRS!

SOME KINDA PLAGUE'S GOING AROUND!

EEEK!

DO SOMETHING WITH YOUR NANOMA-CHINES!

FINE. IF I HAVE TO.

WHAT'S WRONG?

HM?

TUG

TUG

.....

THERE'S A PRETTY PICTURE.

WE'RE PAST THE PEAK.

THAT'S A RELIEF.

IS CULTURAL LEVEL, ANYWAY?

WHAT, EXACTLY...

GUESS THAT'S THEIR RESIDENTIAL DISTRICT.

IT'S IN THE CAVE.

NO IDEA.

AND THE PLANET'S CULTURAL LEVEL WAS RECOGNIZED AS HIGH.

THE PAINTING WAS CRITICALLY ACCLAIMED.

THEY...

DREW *THIS*?!

19

LET'S FINISH THIS QUICKLY AND GET OUT OF HERE.

ALL THE INHABITANTS HAVE ALREADY LEFT.

THIS PLANET'S SCHEDULED FOR REMOVAL TO MAKE WAY FOR A GALACTIC HIGHWAY.

BUT AN OUTSIDER TOOK UP RESIDENCE RECENTLY.

VOLUNTEERS DO ALL KINDS OF JOBS, HUH?

SO WE GOTTA CHASE 'EM OUT.

THERE HE IS.

THIS WHOLE PLANET IS TRASHED.

COVERED IN RUBBLE.

115

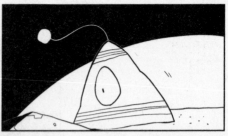

FLASH

WE'RE VOLUNTEERS AND--

UM? EXCUSE ME!

THIS IS NO GOOD.

AH, HELL.

MWAH BLAH!

YAH BLAH!

IF YOU GET HIT WITH THEIR LIGHT, YOUR BRAIN GETS FRIED.

HE'S A MIGONIAN.

AH!

YOU WOULD HAVE BEEN IN TROUBLE IF IT HADN'T BEEN FOR MY NANOMACHINES.

WHAT HAPPENED?

WHAT?

THEN HOW ARE WE SUPPOSED TO NEGOTIATE WITH IT?!

AND THE MIGONIAN LANGUAGE ISN'T IN THE TRANSLATOR.

AND I SPEAK A LITTLE MIGONIAN.

THAT LIGHT DOESN'T WORK ON ME.

I'LL GO CHECK IT OUT.

DON'T JUST GO RUNNIN' UP TO HER.

THAT DOESN'T MEAN SHE TRUSTS YOU YET, THOUGH.

BLAH YAH!

FLASH

TAK

TAK

GREAT!

SHE SAID SHE'S WILLING TO TALK.

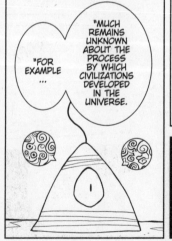

"MUCH REMAINS UNKNOWN ABOUT THE PROCESS BY WHICH CIVILIZATIONS DEVELOPED IN THE UNIVERSE.

"FOR EXAMPLE...

SHE'S CHASING DOWN THE MYSTERIES OF CIVILIZATION IN THE UNIVERSE.

SHE'S A SCIENTIST.

SO IT'S A WOMAN?

WAIT, SHE?!

"AND YET WE SEE COMMONALITIES IN CIVILIZATIONS THAT HAVE NO CONTACT. WHY IS THAT?"

"THE UNIVERSE IS SO LARGE.

"AND THEY'RE VERY SIMILAR.

"THEY'RE FROM TOTALLY DIFFERENT PLACES, BUT THEY WERE MADE AT BASICALLY THE SAME TIME.

"THESE TWO PIECES OF POTTERY COME FROM OPPOSITE ENDS OF THE UNIVERSE.

THAT'S WHAT SHE'S ASKING.

"DO YOU KNOW THE FOURTH-DIMENSION MAN?"

BOING

ISN'T IT BECAUSE THE 4D MAN'S HELPING OUT?

THAT'S..

AH!

GLARE

I'M SORRY! I WON'T TALK ANYMORE!

BUT WE'VE NEVER MET HIM.

HE'S OUR EMPLOYER...

"YOU HAVEN'T..."

LOOK, IT'S DANGEROUS HERE!

WE HAVE TO LEAVE!

ALL INHABITANTS MUST IMMEDIATELY EVACUATE.

THE ENZYME TO DISMANTLE THE PLANET WILL BE DISPERSED IN FIVE MINUTES.

THIS IS A NOTICE TO ALL RESIDENTS.

GAH!

FOUR MINUTES REMAIN- ING!

"I CAN'T ABANDON IT."

"I CAN'T DO THAT.

"EVERYTHING HERE IS A CRITICAL SUBJECT OF STUDY.

120

20

FOUR MINUTES REMAIN-ING!

IS WHAT SHE SAID.

"IF IT MEANS LEAVING BEHIND PRECIOUS RESEARCH MATERIALS ...

"THEN I WILL DIE."

IF WE STAY HERE, WE'RE GOING TO DIE!

THE EVICTION'S STILL NOT FINISHED, THOUGH.

WHAT A SLOPPY PROJECT MANAGER.

WE CAN'T DO THAT!

LET'S JUST LEAVE HER AND GO.

ONCE THE REMOVAL OF THE PLANET STARTS, OUR JOB'S DONE, TOO.

THREE MINUTES REMAIN- ING!

SO, ARE YOU GOING TO TAKE ALL THIS GAR- BAGE WITH US, THEN?

REALLY PRECIOUS?

AND IS ALL OF THIS...

MAYBE THE NANO- MACHINES COULD...

THEY'RE NOT A CURE- ALL.

OF COURSE THEY CAN'T.

HM?

THIS!

A LIMITED-EDITION *PRETTY CARE* FIGURE!

THIS'D COST A PRETTY PENNY AT AUCTION!!

IS IT VALUABLE?

ON THE LEVEL OF A NATIONAL TREASURE.

I COULDN'T EVEN FIND IT IN AKIBA!

SUDDENLY YOU CAN'T SHUT UP.

BLAH

BLAH

BLAH

AND *YO! PRINCESS PRECARE.*

AND *HGUCTTO PRECARE.*

BLAH

AND THIS IS A FIRST-GEN PRECARE.

MY PERSONAL RECOMMEN-DATION IS *HEART PITCH PRECARE.*

DID YOU FIND THIS ON EARTH?

I CAN'T BELIEVE IT'S IN MINT CONDITION!

.....

"SERIOUS-
LY?!"

"COULD
YOU
POSSIBLY
BE...

"AN
EARTH-
LING?"

YEP.
WHY?

THIRTY
SECONDS
REMAIN-
ING!

"EVERYTHING
HERE IS
GARBAGE
COMPARED
WITH AN
EARTHLING!"

"I'VE
ALWAYS
WANTED TO
OBSERVE
A REAL
EARTHLING!"

"LET'S
GET
OUTTA
HERE."

"MY
NAME IS
MINGO-S.

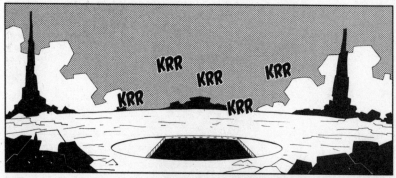

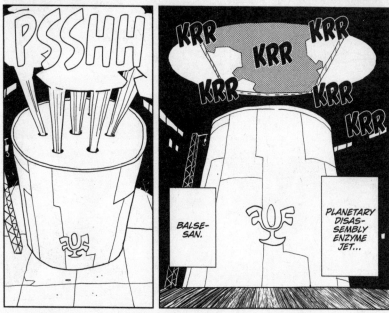

BALSE-SAN.

PLANETARY DISAS-SEMBLY ENZYME JET...

PHEW!

MADE IT BY THE SKIN OF OUR NOSES.

EH?

MIND IF I KEEP THIS?

"NOT AT ALL."

BLAH

THE TRANS-FORMATION ANIMATION IS UNMATCH-ED!

ITS THEMES EXTOL LOVE AND FRIEND-SHIP!

BLAH

BLAH

LOOK!

EVEN ADULTS CAN HAVE FUN WATCHING PRECARE!

BLAH

21

AKKA.

AKKA.

I'M SCARED.

ANOTHER STRANGE GROWN-UP. WHAT'LL WE DO?

JUST IGNORE HER.

LEAVE HER BE.

WHAT, VITA?

A POLITE WAY TO SAY HELLO.

SHF

THAT IS HARDLY...

127

WHAT A RELIEF!

THIS IS MUCH EASIER FOR ME.

CAN CONVERSE VIA **TELEPATHY.**

SHE REALLY IS A SCARY GROWN-UP!

SHE BUTTED INTO OUR CONVERSATION?!

VERY FEW SPECIES IN THE UNIVERSE CAN USE TELEPATHY.

BUT IT'S STRANGE.

IT SEEMS THAT YOU...

TO THINK SUCH **INCREDIBLE CHILDREN** COULD BE BORN OF TWO RACES.

SNUGGLE SNUGGLE

WONDERFUL.

SO YOU'RE A MIX OF EARTHLING AND OVERLORDIAN?

OH HO!

I'D **LOVE** TO STUDY YOU!

WE TAKE A SPIN AROUND EARTH'S OLD ORBIT?

HEY! HOW ABOUT...

BUT THEY'VE BECOME EVEN QUIETER SINCE MINGO-S JOINED US.

THESE KIDS WEREN'T TALKERS TO START WITH...

PLUS, IT COULD BE FUN TO SHOW YOUR KIDS WHERE THEIR DAD'S FROM.

YOU MIGHT REMEMBER SOMETHING, BUB.

SURE.

EARTH'S ORBIT...

SO, THESE ARE THE REMNANTS OF EARTH.

I KNOW IT DOESN'T LOOK LIKE MUCH NOW, BUT...

THIS IS WHERE YOUR DAD WAS BORN AND RAISED!

YUP.

PROHIBITED GROUND?

"I WOULD HAVE LOVED TO VISIT WHILE IT WAS STILL PLANET-SHAPED."

IS WHAT SHE SAID.

"IF ONLY EARTH HADN'T BEEN PROHIBITED GROUND.

130

SOME SNUCK IN ANYWAY.

NO ENTRY WITHOUT THE OKAY OF THE FOURTH-DIMENSION MAN.

DON'T.

I FOUND SOMETHING INTACT!

IT'S WAY BIGGER THAN YOU THINK.

BRING IT IN.

AH!

HUNH.

....

131

JAPANESE PEOPLE HAVE A UNIQUE SENSE OF HUMOR.

FUNNY, RIGHT?

TAKING A BRITISH GUY TO SEE THE STATUE OF LIBERTY IN ODAIBA!

SO?

"SO?" I MEAN...

I WANT TO GO SEE IT!

BUT THE GUNDAM STATUE'S NEAR HERE, RIGHT?!

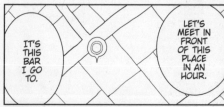

IT'S THIS BAR I GO TO.

LET'S MEET IN FRONT OF THIS PLACE IN AN HOUR.

SO...

SORRY. I GOTTA POP IN AT HOME FOR A BIT.

SEE YOU IN AN HOUR!

'KAY!

THANKS FOR EVERY-THING.

OKAY, GOT IT.

BEEP

22

SO WE BROUGHT THEM TO A NEARBY BUFFET.

WHILE YOU WERE DOWN, THE LITTLE ONES SAID THEY WERE HUNGRY.

WHERE'D EVERYONE GO?

OH YEAH?

'SUP.

YOU'RE AWAKE.

ACTUALLY, I'M HUNGRY, TOO.

OKAY. I'LL GO LOOK FOR THEM.

EVERYONE'S GONE TO GET THEIR PLATES.

136

HERE. THIS IS MY HOME PLANET'S SPECIALTY!

THIS PLACE HAS DISHES FROM ALL OVER THE UNIVERSE!

WE BRITS KNOW BETTER THAN ANYONE IN THE UNIVERSE THE PAIN...

OF HAVING YOUR CUISINE MOCKED.

NAH, LET IT GO...

THIS...

ICK! OH!

THERE YOU ARE!

JUST THOUGHT WE'D ASK.

IT'S FINE.

YOU THEIR GUARDIAN?

SORRY, BUT I CAN'T ACCEPT THESE KIDS' ORDER.

I THOUGHT YOU HAD ALL FOOD IN THE UNIVERSE HERE?!

OH, HELL NO!!

GO ON AND TELL THE NICE MAN WHAT YOU WANT.

NOW...

YOU OKAY?

LOOKS LIKE YOU TOOK SOME SERIOUS DAMAGE.

MOMMY'S COOKING.

......

SLUMP

EARTH?

IF WE HAVE THE DATA, I CAN MAKE IT.

I KNOW!

CAN YOU MAKE EARTH FOOD?

I'M GOING TO TREAT YOU TO THE BEST DISH FROM DADDY'S COUNTRY.

JUST HANG ON.

WHAT'S THAT?

HEH HEH!

TAKE A LOOK!

WE'RE ALL HERE NOW.

HEY, YOU'RE BACK.

FISH AND CHIPS!

THIS IS AN EARTH MEAL.

YOU KIDS...

NO THANKS.

I DON'T LIKE IT.

IT'S NOT SO GREAT.

MUNCH

OH?

140

23

MORNING, BUB.

GOT ANY VOLUNTEER WORK FOR ME?

MORNING, MS. LUMMOX.

I DON'T HAVE ANY WORK, BUT THIS CAME FOR YOU.

ALL YOUR HARD WORK'S BEING RECOGNIZED.

WELL, THAT'S GREAT!

YES!

I'LL FINALLY MEET HIM!

WHAT'S THIS?

IT'S AN INVITATION TO DINNER FROM THE 4D MAN!

THIS INVITE'S FOR THREE PEOPLE.

IT SAYS...

THAT'S THE PLANET.

THAT LOOKS GREAT ON YOU.

GO KNOCK 'EM DEAD.

WAS HE LIVING ON A SMALL, DESERTED PLANET...

ON THE OUTSKIRTS OF THE UNIVERSE THE WHOLE TIME?

NO WONDER NO ONE NOTICED.

THIS PLANET KINDA LOOKS LIKE EARTH.

HUNH.

THERE!

IS NO ONE HERE?

I GUESS HE *IS* THE RECLUSIVE TYPE.

HE LIVES IN A CABIN?

VERY NICE.

FEELS HOMEY.

WE'LL JUST WAIT, THEN.

IS NO ONE HERE?

WHEN YOUR DAD WAS A KID, I USED TO GO TO A SUMMER CAMP IN A PLACE LIKE THIS.

COME ON, NOW!

YOU CAN'T JUST GO AND--

THERE'S FOOD.

I *HAVE* TO TEACH YOU BETTER MANNERS.

IT'S REALLY GOOD!

SLRP

SLRP

VERY THOUGHTFUL, THAT 4D MAN.

HE PROBABLY ARRANGED THINGS TO SUIT ME AS AN EARTHLING.

I SEE!

DIP

MM!

THAT *IS* GOOD!

WE'RE GUESTS HERE. WE MUST BE **POLITE**.

THAT'S A DEFINITE NO.

YANK

THERE'S A TON OF PRESENTS HERE.

YAWN!

NOD NOD

G'NIGHT.

THERE'S A BEDROOM BACK THERE. YOU KIDS GO LIE DOWN.

I'M SURE HE'S JUST REALLY BUSY.

KLATTER
KLATTER

JOLT

SLAM

YEAH.

IT'S BEEN A WHILE SINCE WE SLEPT IN SUCH A NICE PLACE.

A BIG, FLUFFY BLANKET...

KREEE

WHO...?

SOMEONE'S IN THE CLOSET!

THIS IS GOOD WINE.

AH!

24

149

JUICE MADE FROM OPITAKA FRUIT! IT WENT EXTINCT THREE BILLION YEARS AGO.

IT'S GOOD.

SLRP

SLRP

SLRP

SLRP

SO?

UNNNH.

YOU CAN HAVE ANYTHING AND EVERYTHING ON THE ENTIRE AXIS OF TIME IN THE WHOLE UNIVERSE!

IF YOU BECOME MY FAMILY...

I CAN LET YOU SEE YOUR MOM.

AND THAT'S NOT ALL!

IT'S ALREADY MORNING?

I DRANK TOO MUCH.

150

BUT IF THE FOURTH-DIMENSION MAN REALLY DID TAKE THEM...

IT'LL BE NEXT TO IMPOSSIBLE TO FIND THEM.

I'M CALM NOW.

SORRY.

GOOD.

ARGH! SHUT UP!

WHAAAAP

EEEEK!

SHUDDER

LEMME IN YOUR VAGINA A SEC.

SPLOK

SURVEIL-LANCE CAMERAS...

Ah!

WE SHOULD HAVE ATTACHED SURVEILLANCE CAMS TO THE LITTLE ONES.

MS. LUMMOX !!

25

WERE **ABDUCTED**?

AKKA AND VITA...

AND YOU CAN PROJECT IMAGES OF ALL OF SPACE THROUGH MEMORIES, RIGHT?

STARBIAN WOMBS HAVE A SIMPLE WORMHOLE INSIDE THEM.

MM-HMM.

TO PINPOINT WHERE THEY ARE.

I NEED YOUR HELP, MS. LUMMOX...

I WOULD LOVE TO HELP YOU...

I...

THEIR LOCATION FROM MY MEMORIES.

I THINK I CAN PIN DOWN...

MAKES THINGS MORE OF A HASSLE IN ALL KINDS OF WAYS.

THAT...

BUT I'M A VIRGIN.

I'LL TAKE RESPONSIBILITY.

I UNDERSTAND.

MONEY?!

IT'LL BE ABOUT THIS MUCH.

ALL RIGHT!

LET'S SEE.

TAK

TAK

WHAT'S MY WOMB LIKE?

PITCH BLACK.

SPOK

SHE REALLY IS A VIRGIN.

NGH!

I THINK THERE SHOULD BE A LIGHT SWITCH SOME-WHERE.

UGH! SO TIGHT!

NGH!

POP

TUG

THIS IT?

AKKA AND VITA.

THINK ABOUT...

GO AHEAD AND MAKE YOURSELF COMFORTABLE.

VITA.

AKKA.

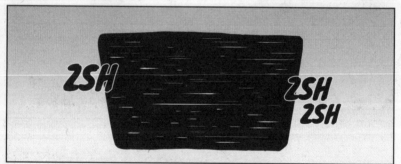

ZSH

ZSH
ZSH

WHAM

MOMMY!

......

IT'S MOMMY!

ONLY I CAN GO THROUGH, SINCE I'M A FOURTH-DIMENSION MAN.

YOU CAN ONLY WATCH THE IMAGES THROUGH A SPACE-TIME HOLE.

UNFORTU-NATELY, YOU CAN'T GO THROUGH.

MOM- MY...

THE IMAGE YOU SEE THROUGH THE HOLE ISN'T THE PAST.

BUT EVEN GETTING A PEEK IS A HUGE DEAL!

IT'S UNMISTAKABLY HER PRESENT.

SO, ARE YOU GRATEFUL?

RIGHT. THAT'S GOOD.

ONE OF THESE DAYS I'M GONNA SUE THEM!

AH! SEE?! LOOK AT THEM, SELLING UNLICENSED MERCH!

THIS IS THE FOURTH-DIMENSION MAN MUSEUM.

HM?

I HATE THAT PLACE.

158

26

DID YOU FIND OUT WHERE THE TWINS ARE?

NO, NOT YET.

BUT I KNOW ONE THING.

THE 4D MAN APPARENTLY CAN'T TAKE THEM AND TRAVEL THROUGH TIME.

YOU ABOUT SATISFIED NOW?

SO?

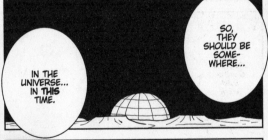

SO, THEY SHOULD BE SOME-WHERE...

IN THE UNIVERSE... IN THIS TIME.

STARE

YOU'RE GOOD AT THAT, RIGHT?

MATH. A MATH THING.

YEAH, WE'RE PRETTY GOOD AT MATH.

BY THE WAY, I ACTUALLY HAVE A FAVOR TO ASK.

EQUATION?

I WANT YOU TO SOLVE THIS LITTLE EQUATION.

IT'S WEIRD THAT YOU'RE ASKING US.

YOU'RE THE FOURTH-DIMENSION MAN, YOU CAN SOLVE IT YOURSELF!

I DON'T WANT TO!

I **HATE** MATH.

LET US SEE HER!

I WANT TO SEE MOMMY!

THIS ISN'T GETTING TO MEET MOMMY.

AND THIS HOLE!

160

NGH.

HNGH.

POP

THERE! IT'S YOUR STUPID DAD!

I'M CHANGING THE CHANNEL!

FINE! IF YOU'RE GOING TO BE LIKE THAT, WE'RE DONE!

BLEEEEH!

LOOK AT THAT GRAY-EYED JERK WITH HIS *WEIRD* HAIR.

DOESN'T HE JUST MAKE YOU SICK?!

THIS BRAT...!

HE'S SAYING THAT *I'VE* GOT WEIRD HAIR?!

I'M GOING FOR A WALK.

YOU TWO DO SOME SOUL-SEARCHING.

VWEEEEN

WE DON'T HAVE TO DO WHAT THAT GUY TELLS US TO.

WE CAN'T SEE MOMMY ANY-MORE.

C'MON, AKKA.

IT'S JUST MATH. LET'S JUST DO IT.

HE'S TOTALLY SKETCHY. AND--

AKKA... VITA...

HE'S WORRIED ABOUT US.

WE'LL GO BACK TO DADDY.

WHAT WILL YOU DO NOW?

SO?

FIRST WE MUST FIND OUT WHERE WE ARE.

WELL, THEN.

GOOD.

BOING

ISN'T THAT...

PRE-CARE?

HM?

IT'S QUITE A MESS.

27

DOO

DOOT DO

I'M A LITTLE TOO EMO- TIONAL.

SORRY FOR GETTING MAD AT YOU.

'SUP!

HE'S BACK!

OH!

FWSH

TRUTH IS, I'VE GOT...

A STORY I'D LOVE FOR YOU TO HEAR.

DA DA

DUMMM

FWIK

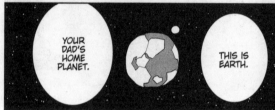

YOUR DAD'S HOME PLANET.

THIS IS EARTH.

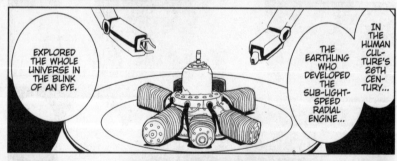

EXPLORED THE WHOLE UNIVERSE IN THE BLINK OF AN EYE.

THE EARTHLING WHO DEVELOPED THE SUB-LIGHT-SPEED RADIAL ENGINE...

IN THE HUMAN CULTURE'S 26TH CENTURY...

THERE WERE **NO OTHER** INTELLIGENT BEINGS IN THE **ENTIRE UNIVERSE.**

AND THEY DISCOVERED...

166

EVENTUALLY, THERE WAS ONLY **ONE EARTHLING** LEFT.

THE INSTANT THEY REALIZED THIS, ALL HUMAN DEVELOPMENT STOPPED.

THEY WERE ALL ALONE.

THE BIRTH RATE DROPPED, AND THE POPULATION GRADUALLY DECREASED.

THEY COMMITTED SUICIDE?

FWP

WHAT HAPPENED TO THE LAST EARTH PERSON?

OKAY! QUIZ TIME!

THE POWERFUL CONSCIOUS-NESS OF THE UNIVERSE FORCED THEM TO LIVE.

A POWER TO PRESERVE THE SPECIES WAS AT WORK.

AS A RESULT ...

NOT ONLY WERE THEY THE LAST PERSON ON EARTH, THEY WERE THE LAST PERSON IN THE UNIVERSE.

BUT IT WAS NO USE.

THEY *TRIED*.

CLOSE!

THEY TRANSFORMED INTO THE FOURTH-DIMENSION MAN.

IT WAS ME!

YUP!

GEH HEH

HEH!

FIDDLED WITH MY DNA A LITTLE, AND PUT CREATURES ON RANDOM PLANETS.

I JUST WENT BACK TO THE BIRTH OF THE UNIVERSE...

IT WAS EASY WORK.

I DECIDED TO CREATE MANY CIVILIZATIONS IN THE UNIVERSE.

REBORN AS THE FOURTH-DIMENSION MAN...

IF I FAILED, I COULD DO IT OVER HOWEVER MANY TIMES I WANTED.

IF I WAS LUCKY, I'D FIND NEW INTELLIGENT BEINGS.

THEN I JUST HAD TO MOVE A BILLION YEARS OR SO FORWARD IN TIME.

I CREATED A REALITY BUSTLING WITH TENS OF THOUSANDS OF CIVILIZATIONS!

BUT, STARTING FROM A LONELY UNIVERSE OF NOTHING BUT EARTHLINGS...

IT TOOK A DIZZYING AMOUNT OF TIME...

AND THAT'S HOW I REMADE THE UNIVERSE.

BUT LATELY, I FEEL LIKE I'M AT A DEAD END, CREATIVELY.

I'VE BEEN WORKING SO HARD.

SLUMP

......

YOU REALLY ARE GODLIKE.

WOW.

I KNOW, RIGHT?!

I WANT TO SEE A DIFFERENT WORLD.

SURROUNDED ONLY BY MY OWN IDEAS, MY CREATIVE URGE IS FADING.

IT'S AS THOUGH I'M TRAPPED IN MY OWN *MINECRAFT* WORLD.

YOU CAN'T MOVE BETWEEN UNIVERSES UNLESS YOU'RE A **FIFTH-DIMENSION** PERSON.

BUT I'M JUST A PLAIN OL' **FOURTH-DIMENSION** MAN.

THERE ARE PLENTY OF UNIVERSES BESIDES THIS ONE IN THE MULTIVERSE.

THAT'S RIGHT! I WANT TO EXPLORE *OTHER* UNIVERSES!

GLOOM

SO SAD!

IF YOU DO, I CAN GO TO OTHER UNIVERSES.

COULD YOU SOLVE THIS EQUATION FOR ME?

THAT'S WHERE THE FAVOR COMES IN.

WELL...

I GUESS WE COULD.

WHAT DO YOU THINK?

......

170

28

THAT'S *DEFINITELY* PRECARE.

SO? YOU GET A LOCATION?

POP

THE SHIFT IN CHARACTER DESIGNS CAUSED QUITE AN UPROAR AMONGST DEDICATED FANS FOR A LONG TIME, BUT RECENTLY--

SHE'S SUPER RARE, TOO.

SHE WAS ONLY IN THE MOVIE VERSION.

BLAH

BLAH BLAH

UH-HUH.

I'M PRETTY SURE EARTH'S SATELLITE IS STILL THERE.

MAYBE IT'S THE MOON?

NOT YET.

BUT A PLACE WHERE A PRECARE FIGURE COULD FALL...

IT WOULDN'T BE STRANGE IF EARTH'S GARBAGE WASHED UP THERE.

ACTUALLY, THE MOON...

DID I SAY SOMETHING STRANGE?

OH DEAR! I'M SORRY.

THERE AREN'T ANY DIRECT WORMHOLES.

IT'LL TAKE TIME TO GET TO THE REMAINS OF EARTH FROM HERE.

BUT...

I KNOW ANOTHER ROUTE.

WELL, IN THAT CASE...

172

173

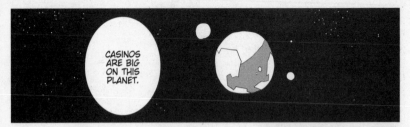

CASINOS ARE BIG ON THIS PLANET.

YOU CAN FIND UNDERGROUND GAMBLING PARLORS ON THE BACK-STREETS.

WELL, IF IT ISN'T BUB!

HM?

HOW'S IT GOING?

THIS PLACE IS MEMBERS ONLY.

SCRAM.

SO YOU'VE GOT SOME CLOUT IN THE UNDERWORLD, HM?

TA.

GO ON IN.

174

THE MAFIA HAS ACCESS TO DARK WORMHOLES THAT AREN'T PUBLIC.

RIGHT THIS WAY.

YOU GOT ANY WORMHOLES THAT GO TO EARTH?

ONLY ONE OF THESE THREE HOLES LEADS TO EARTH.

IT'S A GAMBLE FROM HERE.

AGAIN ?!

WHERE YOU'RE FORCED INTO HARD LABOR FOR A YEAR.

THE OTHER TWO GO TO THE MINING PLANET...

BE CAREFUL.

MS. LUMMOX, YOU WAIT HERE.

GURK

WHOEVER GETS THE RIGHT ONE, TAKE CARE OF MY KIDS.

WE EACH TAKE ONE.

WE'VE GOT NO CHOICE.

ROGER THAT.

GOT IT.

29

THE MOON?

IS THIS...

ZZZNK

WELL, IT'S ALL ON ME NOW.

LOOKS LIKE I WON.

OH, WHOOP-EE.

KIIIIDS!

HEY!

DUNNO IF I'M GONNA BE ABLE TO FIND THEM...

IT MIGHT BE A SATELLITE, BUT IT'S PRETTY BIG.

178

A SCIENTIFIC INVESTIGATION.

MINGOS!

WHAT ARE YOU DOING HERE?

WHAT HAPPENED TO THE TWINS?

WITHOUT JUNK, WE CAN'T TALK, HUH?

HYOOOO

HANG ON!

AH!

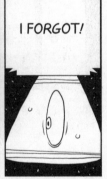

I FORGOT!

SKRK

SKRK

SKRK

179

OOH!

WE SOLVED IT.

KAK KAK

I'M FINALLY GOING FROM THE FOURTH-DIMENSION TO THE FIFTH!

ALL RIGHT!

NOW I CAN GO TO ANOTHER UNIVERSE!

BWAAN

BUT BEFORE THAT...

THANKS!

THERE'S SOMETHING I GOTTA DO.

TAKE CARE ON THE OTHER SIDE.

CONGRATS!

CLAP

CLAP

WE CAN'T LET YOU GO!

NO!

YANK

SHUDDER

WHERE ARE YOU GOING?

I'VE GOT A BAD FEELING!

GAH!

MAYBE YOU GET THAT FROM YOUR MOM.

GOOD INSTINCTS.

YEAH!

VITA, WE DEFINITELY CAN'T LET GO!

Earth - Odaiba

182

IT'S HUGE.

WHOA!

HE'S STARING AT THE ODAIBA GUNDAM WITH THAT DOPEY LOOK ON HIS FACE.

LOOK AT THAT GUY.

FROM BEFORE WE WERE BORN.

IT'S DADDY.

I BETTER HEAD OVER TO WHERE WE'RE MEETING.

WHOOPS!

DiverCity Tokyo

WELP!

LOOKS LIKE IT'S HERE.

SO I DESTROYED EARTH. NORMALLY, THE FERTILIZATION RATE BETWEEN AN OVER-LORDIAN AND AN EARTHLING IS EXTREMELY LOW.

SO I BOOSTED THE ODDS BY GIVING YOUR DAD THE DRIVE TO PRESERVE HIS SPECIES.

LET'S BAIL BEFORE WE GET DRAGGED INTO THIS.

SSP

IF I HADN'T DESTROYED EARTH, YOU TWO WOULDN'T HAVE BEEN BORN.

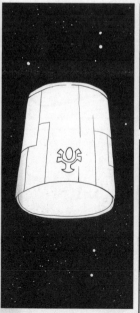

WHAT'S THAT?

HEY.

Venus Fort

YO!

FOUND YA!

WHAT IS THAT THING?

SO THEN... THAT'S A SPACE-SHIP?!

A-AN ALIEN?!

ACK!

YOU'RE GONNA GET IN THIS LIFE POD.

OKAY, BUDDY.

THIS IS SO ANNOYING!

YEAH, YEAH, WHAT-EVER.

WHAT-EVS. YOU'LL BE FINE.

MAYBE THAT WAS TOO STRO-NG.

HMYAH.

KA-ZAP

JUST GET IN.

EEK!

YOU GOTTA PULL YOUR WEIGHT ON THIS ONE.

I'M COUNTING ON YOU!

HAH!

HAH!

Frontier planet Kohyahyah

WE GOTTA HAVE FAITH IN HIM.

HOPE HOPPER'S DOING OKAY...

187

WHEW!

UHM...

WHOA. BUB?

HM?

WHAT'S WRONG?

WHAT ARE YOU TALKING ABOUT?

YOU LOOK LIKE THE FOURTH-DIMENSION MAN...

GROSS!

UGH!

TOTALLY NOT CUTE!

LOOK.

AAA-AAH!

IN ABOUT **THREE HUNDRED THOUSAND YEARS,** THIS HEAVY CLOUD OF GAS COLLAPSES AND THE FIRST STARS ARE BORN.

AND THE CREATION OF ONE SPECIFIC SOLAR SYS-TEM'S ANOTHER **FIVE BILLION** YEARS AWAY.

MOMENTS AFTER CREATION, THE HAZY UNIVERSE.

THIS IS THE START OF EVERY-THING.

WHERE ARE WE?

REALITY... IS EMPTY AND LONELY AFTER ALL.

EARTHLINGS WERE NOTHING BUT ANOMALOUS GARBAGE.

IN THE END...

BUT ONLY THERE.

EVENTUALLY, LIFE WILL MULTIPLY AND THRIVE ON THE THIRD PLANET THERE.

FOR ITS ENTIRE LIFE SPAN OF 160 BILLION YEARS, THAT'S THE ONLY LIFE THIS UNIVERSE WILL PRODUCE.

I'LL RESET EVERYTHING ABOUT THIS GARBAGE CAN OF A WORLD!

BEFORE I LEAVE FOR ANOTHER UNIVERSE...

THAT'S WHY I MADE A DECISION!

RUB

RUB

WE'RE ALL OUT OF CLUES.

IT'S HOPELESS.

I'VE FAILED YOU, BUB.

WHAT ARE YOU DOING HERE?!

HUH?!

NOT TRUE.

I DON'T KNOW HOW IT HAPPENED...

BUT BUB SUDDENLY AWAKENED AS A FOURTH-DIMENSION MAN.

AND YOU'VE BEEN DESIGNATED TO TAKE HIS PLACE.

THE CURRENT FOURTH-DIMENSION MAN IS LIKELY ABOUT TO ABANDON THIS UNIVERSE.

THAT MUST BE IT!

HMM.

YOU KNOW SOME-THING?

YOU REALLY ARE A FOURTH-DIMENSION MAN.

YOU'RE TALKING WITH MINGO-S...

SERI-OUSLY?! NO ONE TOLD ME THIS!

YOU CAN'T GO AGAINST THE UNIVERSE'S WILL.

I'LL GIVE IT A GO.

YOU SHOULD BE ABLE TO FIND THE TWINS NOW.

SOME-WHERE AROUND HERE?

BOMF

192

I CAN DO WHAT I WANT WITH IT! THIS IS MY UNIVERSE!

WHAP

OW! THAT HURTS!

QUIT IT, YOU STUPID BRATS!

BAP

GRAB

YOINK

194

HANG ON!

MINGO-S?!

SIZZ SIZZ

I REMEMBER.

. . .

KA-RELLEN ...

THAT LIGHTNING **KILLED** KARELLEN.

AND SHE...

I WAS HIT WITH THAT LIGHTNING.

RIGHT BEFORE THE EARTH WAS DESTROYED ...

EVEN IF IT'S TRUE, YOU DON'T TO SAY IT!

YOU BASTARD!

AFTER LOSING THEIR MOM, THE TWINS WOULD GET SICK OF THEIR **WORTHLESS DAD** AND CLING TO ME.

AND I KNEW...

SHE WAS TOO SMART. I HAD TO TAKE CARE OF HER BEFORE SHE FIGURED OUT MY PLAN.

SQUEEZE

DADDY'S NOT WORTHLESS!

KIDS...

AND NOW WE REALLY LOVE OUR HARD BED...

WE GOT TO SEE ALL KINDS OF STUFF IN ALL THESE DIFFERENT PLACES.

WE HAD FUN TRAVELING WITH YOU.

AND THE SMELLY ENGINE ROOM!

HE'S HARMLESS NOW.

HE'S TOTALLY FRIED.

POKE

THAT'S A RELIEF!

MINGO-S IS OKAY.

WHAT'LL WE DO WITH HIM?

WE'LL TOSS HIM IN FRONT OF THE FOURTH-DIMENSION MAN MUSEUM.

THUD

MAY THE MIGHTY FOURTH-DIMENSION MAN WATCH OVER YOU.

HERE.

CLANK

OH, POOR DEAR.

DADDY, DID YOU BECOME A FOURTH-DIMENSION MAN?

APPAR-ENTLY.

I'M JUST GLAD YOU'RE SAFE.

C'MERE.

CAN WE SAVE MOMMY WITH THIS POWER?

SHFF

US, TOO.

BOTH OF THEM HAVE EARTHLING BLOOD... SO MAYBE THAT'S IT?

WHAT'S THAT ABOUT?

IT'S POSSIBLE TO REVIVE THE EARTH WITHOUT USING YOUR POWERS, YOU KNOW.

HOW-EVER!

GOD OR WHO-EVER...

BUT IF THERE'S SOMEONE IN THIS UNIVERSE WHO MADE EARTH-LINGS...

I DON'T KNOW.

I THINK THAT'S THE ONLY BEING WHO SHOULD HAVE POWER OVER LIFE AND DEATH.

WE UNDER-STAND.

YEAH.

199

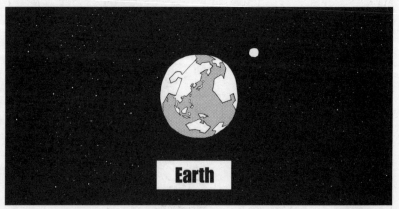

Earth

How Many Light-Years to Babylon?   END

END